CW00454834

For Catherine and Holly
Thanks for sharing

"One of my favorite scenes in the Gospels is when Jesus explains salvation to Nicodemus. Without a hint of awkwardness or hesitation, he employs the metaphor of female reproduction: womb, water, and blood. Yet, in the church today, the female reproductive cycle is still regarded as taboo to speak of, let alone to ponder in relation to our faith. I'm deeply grateful that Rachel Jones has endeavored to dignify what God has architected and to help us consider what we might learn from that design. As the prevailing culture dismantles the categories of male and female before our eyes, Rachel shows us how precious the gift of our female biology is, and all the more for the theology it illustrates."

Jen Wilkin, Author, *None Like Him* and *Ten Words to Live By*

"Clever, theologically robust, and with real depth, *A Brief Theology of Periods* digs into what it means to be a woman from a fascinating angle. This is, though, not just for women—everyone will find this book illuminating in a profoundly helpful way."

Linda Allcock, Author, *Deeper Still*

"I admit that I've never viewed 'that time of the month' with anything but disdain. Therefore I was a bit skeptical of a book addressing periods through the eyes of theology. But Rachel Jones did the impossible. In a humorous and honest (yet tasteful) way, Rachel helps reshape our naturally negative view of periods to one that is shaped by the gospel and God's good purposes in every aspect of life—yes, even in this."

Sarah Walton, Author, *Hope When It Hurts*

"This is a fantastic theological reflection on menstruation (yes, really), full of pastoral insight and encouragement. It's great to have someone address this important subject: even better that Rachel has addressed it so well. I'm sure it will be a blessing to many women—but let me also urge you to read it if you're a husband, father, brother, pastor or (male) friend. If you want to care well for half your family, half your church and half the world, then this subject should matter to you."

Tim Chester, Faculty Member, Crosslands Training;
Author, *Enjoying God*

"I cried in my office when I read the opening pages of Rachel's book. She described a narrative that had dominated my life, though I had stuffed it down deep in my psyche in the file of things you endure without thought. From huddling in misery at a youth sleepover because my cramps were so bad I couldn't unfurl to my last multi-week periods in my forties that only stopped with a hysterectomy, my cycle dominated my days for thirty years. Rachel reminds us that our periods are not separate from our spiritual life. Our cycles cannot be separated from our person or the Spirit who indwells us. She offers a theology of a woman's body from Scripture that is thought provoking and practical. Our bodies matter!"

Wendy Alsup, Author, *Companions in Suffering* and
Is the Bible Good for Women?

"Embarrassing. Messy. Uncomfortable. Gross. Periods can be all of these things and more, but this book is none of them. A witty, insightful introduction to the marvels of menstruation and how our periods can point us to God. Yes, really."

Jennie Pollock, Author, *If Only*

"Surely an essential part of loving others is understanding and empathy. If you're a man and you desire to love like that, it's a very short step to seeing that you need to read this book. I'll now be a little better informed about an area that is so much a part of the lives of the women in my life. As ever, Rachel Jones writes with a wry smile on her face and an amazing ability to apply the Bible to our lives. I loved the combination of humour and theology."

Rico Tice, Senior Minister, All Souls Langham Place, London;
Author, *Faithful Leaders*

"Most Christians throughout history—regardless of time or culture—have had one oft-neglected thing in common: periods. In this energetic and helpful book, Rachel Jones thinks theologically about the quiet drumbeat of female experience and orients us toward God in the midst of things that might feel painful, shameful, or emotionally charged. Whether periods play a big part in your life or no part at all, you will find biblical wisdom in this book that will help you navigate your own experiences or support those you love in theirs."

Rebecca McLaughlin, Author, *Confronting Christianity;*
Co-founder, *Vocable Communications*

RACHEL JONES

A BRIEF THEOLOGY OF PERIODS

(YES, REALLY)

thegoodbook
COMPANY

A Brief Theology of Periods (Yes, Really)
© The Good Book Company, 2021

Published by:
The Good Book Company

thegoodbook.com | thegoodbook.co.uk
thegoodbook.com.au | thegoodbook.co.nz | thegoodbook.co.in

Unless indicated, all Scripture references are taken from the Holy Bible, New International Version. Copyright © 2011 Biblica, Inc. Used by permission.

All rights reserved. Except as may be permitted by the Copyright Act, no part of this publication may be reproduced in any form or by any means without prior permission from the publisher.

Rachel Jones has asserted her right under the Copyright, Designs and Patents Act 1988 to be identified as author of this work.

Cover design by Jennifer Phelps | Design and art direction by André Parker

ISBN: 9781784986216 | Printed in the UK

Contents

So Many Reasons

Let me run you through a conversation I've had on numerous occasions since starting out on this project.

Person A [an unsuspecting and well-meaning church member, let's say]: *So, are you writing any books at the moment?*

Me [deliberately vague]: *Well… err… yeah, I guess I am.*

Person A [blissfully unaware of what they're about to walk into]: *Oh great! What's it about?*

Me [with a deep breath and a smile]: *It's about periods.*

Person A: *Like "periods of time" periods?*

Me: *No, periods periods. You know, with blood.*

Person A [stunned]: *Oh…*

[Pause]

Why?!

Why write a Christian book about periods?

So many reasons…

1. They're a part of normal life

Let's start with the obvious: for roughly 50% of the population, for a large section of our lives, periods are a regular reality. 400-500 times in your lifetime—and for 60 days of the year—you're on your period. To a greater or lesser extent, our menstrual cycle shapes our schedule, what we do and how we feel in the course of any given month—even beyond that particular "time of the month".

For most women, periods are annoying and inconvenient. For some women, they are utterly debilitating (more on that in chapter 2). Either way, if you have periods (or if you don't have periods when you're meant to have periods), then they are a fact of life you cannot avoid.

2. The Bible speaks to all of life

Here's another statement which I hope is just as obvious to you: if you're a Christian, there is not one area of life which can be divorced from your faith. There is not one area that God declares himself uninterested in. If the biggest reality underpinning the universe is that Jesus is Lord and that he died to bring us into an eternal relationship with God, then that should shape how we think about all the *other* realities of our day-to-day existence.

From how we use social media to what we eat, where we work, how much we sleep, who we sleep with and what we wear... all of it, on some level (and to varying degrees) can be thought through *theologically*. That is, it can all be fitted into the big story of what God is doing in the world and how he calls us to live in the world.

The incredible thing about God's word is that it *truly* speaks to all of life. And there are plenty of great books out there that show you what the Bible says when it comes to social media, work, leisure, sex, beauty or friendship. But periods? Not so much. Yet if Christians are squeamish about this, that's not because the Bible is: it's gritty and real. And it speaks about real life at the sharp end: about pain and endurance, about shame and struggle, about disappointment and loss and love. And it talks *a lot* about blood.

So if periods are part of life, and the Bible speaks to all of life, then God can—indeed, God *wants to*—speak into how we experience them. He wants to affirm us and encourage us and challenge us as we seek to walk with Jesus on every day of the month.

3. Life speaks the gospel to us

It works the other way round too. It's not just that the Bible speaks to us about real life; real life speaks to us about the gospel. "Consider the ravens…" says Jesus: "Consider how the wild flowers grow…" (Luke 12 v 24, 27). *Look around,* says Jesus, *and see how God.…*

And while, ok, he didn't *quite* say, *Consider your periods,* the general principle is that we live in a created world that speaks of its Creator (more on this in chapter 1). So considering our periods is what we're going to do here.

This means periods don't *just* have to be something we endure or put up with. They can also be something positive: something that reminds us of the spiritual realities that underpin our existence, and that presents us with an opportunity to fix our eyes on the Lord Jesus.

I know that probably sounds *really* weird. Yes, it may be that I've been sitting in a room thinking about periods for just a few months too long. But, bear with me. It'll be worth it.

4. The Bible talks about periods

Points 1 to 3 have hopefully persuaded you to read on. But all those reasons were before we even get to pointing out that the Bible does talk about periods specifically.

My personal favourite period mention is a bizarre incident in Genesis 31, where Rachel steals the household gods that belong to her father, Laban, before going on the run with her husband, Jacob. When Laban catches up with the couple, he accuses them of stealing and starts to search their belongings. Rachel is sitting on the place where the idols are hidden, and when Laban searches through the tent she says to him, "Don't be angry, my lord, that I cannot stand up in your presence; I'm having my period"—with the result that Laban "searched but could not find the household gods" (Genesis 31 v 35). Which is pretty sneaky. But when your husband announces that anyone who's stolen your dad's household gods will be put to death, and they're right there in your camel saddle, what else can you do except sit tight and blame "the way of women" (as the ESV so elegantly translates it)?

But that's about as fun as it gets for menstruating women in the Bible. You might already know that women on their period were considered unclean in the Old Testament (Leviticus 15, a passage we'll grapple with in detail in chapter 3) and that having sex while on your period was an absolute no-no (Leviticus 18 v 19).

So it's no surprise that when people talk about periods in our culture today, if religion gets a mention, it's almost always in negative terms. Christianity is blamed for perpetuating centuries of taboos around periods. Words like "puritanical" are used as an insult.

So… is Christianity the bad guy here? How do we make sense of what the Bible says about periods when it jars with the way 21st-century Westerners see things?

5. If we don't look to the Bible to shape our thinking, our culture will shape our thinking instead

Let's be honest: your pastor probably won't be preaching about periods anytime soon. But there are plenty of other people who *will*.

The last few years have seen an increasing number of voices talking about periods in our culture. There's been an explosion of books and podcasts on the subject. Periods are becoming increasingly visible on TV and in movies and advertising. In 2019 the "drop of blood" emoji finally made it onto our messaging apps, and a year later periods were even given their own Pantone colour (red, naturally). Social media is full of lively conversations on issues such as period poverty, the tampon tax, free bleeding, environmentally-friendly menstrual-hygiene choices, health inequalities, the gender pain gap, specific conditions such as endometriosis, and what to call the people who have periods—women, menstruators, or something else?

Here's the thing: nothing we read or watch or listen to is ideologically neutral—it's all subtly (or not so subtly) telling us how to think and how to act. Everything comes with its own implicit messages about what's good, what's bad and what's important in life in general.

So if we're not proactive about thinking *Christianly* about a subject, then we'll just end up having our thinking shaped by what the world tells us. And while that's rarely going to be all wrong, it's not going to be all right, either. For Christians, it's Scripture which is meant to define the good, the bad and the important. We need to learn to think critically about culture—to get equipped to sift truth from error, to identify wisdom amid the folly, and to have all our thinking shaped by God's word.

This is true for any subject. But periods are one that comes knocking for us pretty regularly—both on our screens and, well, in our knickers.

And hey—if you are a pastor, or a husband, dad, or brother in Christ who's reading this because you want to love your sisters, well then, *thank you*. I hope this book will help with that too.

6. A book about periods is a way of thinking about a whole load of other things

I'm imagining that you might have picked up this book out of sheer curiosity. "A Christian book about periods? Now *that's* one I haven't seen before."

But now that I've got you this far, I want to take you on a journey in thinking about a whole lot more than periods. Don't get me wrong: we'll be thinking plenty about that time of the month. But that touches on so many bigger questions too. We'll see how periods springboard us into thinking about what it means to have a body or to experience mortality. We'll ask: what even is a woman anyway? We'll grapple with questions about how God speaks, the purpose of humanity and the meaning of life. We'll think about how we spend our time now and what we'll spend our time doing for eternity.

And all from the starting point of periods.

7. It was a game of publishing brinkmanship that (arguably) went horribly wrong

I know writing a Christian book about periods might make me sound kind of strange. But I'm not that strange really. I'm writing this as someone who has both periods and a penchant for pushing the envelope. When I first floated this idea, I didn't think anyone would take it seriously. Then I wanted to see if I *could* get people to take it seriously. And then they did take it seriously—for all the reasons I've just stated above.

And now, a year or two later, here we all are—my name is on a Christian book about periods, and you're holding it.

So, welcome.

QUEUE UP THE CAVEATS

But before we go any further, there are a few things to acknowledge up front.

First, there is a *huge* variety in the way that we experience periods. This is true on a physical level. Even something as basic as the notion that the average cycle is 28 days masks a great deal of variation—a study by University College London and the Natural Cycles app found that only 13% of women actually have a 28-day cycle. Periods can be more or less regular, more or less lengthy, more or less heavy, more or less painful and more or less emotionally intense. Or maybe, for one of a variety of reasons, you don't have periods at all.

And how we *feel* about our periods will vary so much too, depending on our culture, family background, age, and where we're at in life. Periods are going to mean vastly different things to you if you're 18 and about to leave home, or 28 and trying for a baby, or 48 and single.

But whatever your experience, I'm hoping that you'll find something life-giving and thought-provoking in the pages that follow. Not because I have the insight required to perceive and address all those different situations specifically—I really don't, and I certainly haven't—but because we're simply going to look at what Scripture says. And as I've said, I'm confident that the Bible speaks to all of life for all of us—whatever life looks like right now.

Second, this is not a women's health book. There are lots of fascinating ones out there, several of which I've enjoyed reading and which you might too. While we'll look a bit at the biology, we'll only do that in so far as it helps us with the theology. I am not a doctor, and I'm not here to tell you whether what you experience is normal, or healthy, or whatever. If you are *at all* concerned that something might not be quite right with your menstrual cycle—or if your periods prevent you from doing the normal things you need to do in a day—can I encourage you to *please* talk to a doctor. Please. And while I can't give you a medical consultation, I like to think that by the end of this book you might be a little bit less squeamish and embarrassed—and a little more confident and hopeful—about periods in general, and therefore about seeking help if you've got particular concerns.

Third, some things in this book may be hard to read. In fact, some of it may even offend you. I've tried to take the issues seriously without taking myself too seriously, but we can't get past the fact that what the Bible says about us (and our bodies) isn't always what we want to hear. But if we're ready to hear it anyway—if we're ready to step into the light—then we will find it to be liberating; because, more than anything, I want to point you to Jesus: the one who came to bring freedom and hope and life in all its fullness (John 10 v 10). In him there is no condemnation—only grace.

Why write a book about periods? Because for every politely baffled church member I've told about this book—for every conversation that's run like the one on page 9—I've met more women whose eyes light up and who say, "Really? I *love* it. I can't wait."

And if that's you, then I'm so glad you're reading. This is going to be fun. At the very least, it'll be more fun than actually having your period—but since that doesn't set the bar very high, I don't think they'll put that on the back of the book. And while reading this won't make the experience of having your period more fun, I am hoping it will make it more positive. Think of what follows as an adventure for the theologically curious. This book is for women who bleed and women who have stopped; it's for you if you hate your period and struggle through every one, and it's for you if you breeze through your period and have never really given them a second thought.

Whoever you are, my aim is that you reach the end of this book celebrating who God has made you and how God has saved you, and the fact that he speaks liberating and positive truth into all of life's experiences—even the bloody ones.

CHAPTER ONE

So Much Potential

Your body is incredible. All of it.

And more precisely, for the purposes of this book, your female body is incredible.

Of course, it's quite possible that you've never really appreciated *quite* how incredible your body is "down there", because no one's ever really told you. You might have been taught about it in school, but that kind of education varies greatly and can often be pretty minimal—so much so that in a survey by the charity Plan, one in four girls in the UK said that they didn't feel prepared for their first period (see Lynn Enright, *Vagina*, page 103). My poor mother thought she was dying because no one had thought to warn her what would happen. My friend Maya knew exactly what was happening, but refused to admit it and went about the rest of her day in denial.

Alternatively, it might have been that your teachers said all the right things during "the puberty presentation" but that—like another friend of mine—you just passed out in the middle of it. (She's always claimed it was the animated moving diagrams that pushed her over the edge.) Or maybe all that was just a very long time ago.

So if, like me, you're in need of a refresh—or of being convinced that the statement with which I began this chapter is in any way true—here is what happens when you have your period. Consider this your invitation to a 28-day(ish) hormonal cocktail party that—whether you're aware of it or not—you're hosting in your body every month.

HORMONAL COCKTAIL PARTY

Days 1-6(ish): The first day of your period is regarded as "Day One" of your cycle, which is helpful, since that's the moment we can all see with certainty. We normally think of the stuff we can see as blood, but it also contains endometrial cells and uterine tissue, as the lining of your womb sheds itself in the absence of a pregnancy.

Meanwhile, the party in one of your two ovaries is really getting going. The relevant guest here is follicle-stimulating hormone (FSH), which arrives from the pituitary gland all the way up in your brain. When she bowls in, she gets the follicles all riled up for a competition (like drinking games, or, in Christian ovaries, board games). The prize is to be the bearer of the next egg to be sent out into the big wide womb for a chance of fertilisation. Only the biggest and best will win.

Days 7-13: This is the second part of phase one of your menstrual cycle (the "follicular phase"). By the end of your period, next month's winning follicle has been selected. The follicle releases oestrogen, which tells the pituitary gland in your brain to stop producing FSH so that the other, lesser follicles stop growing while the dominant follicle continues to mature (increasing in size from under 4mm to up to 25mm). Oestrogen causes the lining of the womb to thicken and stimulates the production of cervical fluid to aid conception, as well as tending to make us feel more positive and sociable. Oestrogen's a feel-good party guest who brings a lot of fun—telling jokes, smiling at the boys and leading the charge to the dancefloor.

Day 14: Ovulation. Oestrogen produced by the ovary invites lutenising hormone (LH) from the pituitary gland to join the party, which in turn stimulates more oestrogen until... Voila! The egg is cooked to perfection in its follicle oven. It's served up into the fallopian tube where, for around 12-24 hours, it remains viable for an encounter with a visiting sperm.

Day 15 onwards: We're now into phase two of our menstrual cycle (the "luteal phase"). Back at the ranch (err, ovary), the empty follicle becomes a gland which, prompted by the LH from the brain, produces another hormone, progesterone. Progesterone is a nurturing soul who's there to support a pregnancy if you need her to, but she's got great health benefits too, like building bone tissue. She's the kind of hormone who would prefer a "gathering" to a house party, and who can sometimes be found crying in the bathroom.

At this stage the lining of the uterus continues to thicken to around 18mm (in other words, more than four times thicker than it was at the end of your period. That's a lot of layers of red paint).

Day 20 onwards: Progesterone and oestrogen levels start to drop off, like guests gradually drifting away from a party. Right on cue, the prostaglandins show up. Like parents who come home to find the tail end of a teenage house party, the prostaglandins tell the endometrium (womb lining) to clear out. And we're left with a bit of mess to clear up. (But hey— did you hear there's another party just starting up in the ovary on the other side? Go check it out!)[1]

500 TIMES

So that's what's going on inside you, every single month— who knew, huh?!

Well, I didn't, for one. Before writing this book, despite having experienced around 200 cycles of my own, I didn't know about 80% of this. My menstrual cycle is a finely tuned, intricately balanced system featuring hormones that work in harmony as they rise and fall, stop things and start things, and "talk" to each other… all without me having to tell them to. My ovary doesn't wait for a conscious order before it gets cracking on next month's egg. It's doing its thing, month after month, approximately 400-500 times in my lifetime, largely unbeknownst to me.

It is, frankly, remarkable.

And that's just one set of organs and glands! Our bodies contain a whole web of intricate systems that keep us alive and healthy—the circulatory system, the digestive system, the

---

1 This section owes much, in content and style, to chapter 2 of Maisie Hill's book *Period Power* (pages 26-46). Her explanation of the biology of the menstrual cycle is the clearest I've found—check it out for more detail.

immune system and so on. And we don't have to understand them in order to benefit from them.

In that sense, life in the body is the most incredible gift. We didn't design it, didn't buy it and don't consciously control most of it, and many of us don't know that much about it.

But it's ours. It's us. And it's incredible.

WHY PERIODS?

So that's *how* periods happen. The obvious next question is *why?*

Periods are, when you think about it, seemingly nonsensical from an evolutionary point of view. They're resource-heavy—all that endometrium takes a lot of nutrients to build up. Apart from humans, only a small and curious selection of other mammals shed it externally: some types of primates, as well as bats, elephant shrews and the spiny mouse. Most other mammals sensibly reabsorb the endometrium back into the body.

Scientists have various theories as to why it would be advantageous for our bodies to bleed for a week every month—but they're, well, theories. Why do we have periods? An honest scientist will tell you that we don't really know for sure.

But the Bible would tell you that you *can* know. Or rather, it says that our bodies—both in their design and their detail—are intended to send us a message.

This is the principle that theologians call "general revelation". The idea is that all created things *reveal* something about our Creator. Scripture claims that "the heavens declare the glory of God" (Psalm 19 v 1); and that "since the creation of the world God's invisible qualities—his eternal power and divine nature—have been clearly seen, being understood from what has been made" (Romans 1 v 20). "What has been made" includes your body. As part of creation you are a small but wonderful walking advertisement of your Creator's glory—his "God-ness".

So our bodies tell us something about *God*. They point to the existence of someone beyond us—a Designer and a Giver—and, as we'll see through this chapter, reveal something about the extent of his power and the goodness of his character. When the psalmist looks at the cosmos, and mankind's place in it, he proclaims, "Lord, our Lord, how majestic is your name in all the earth" (Psalm 8 v 1, 9).

Not only that but our bodies tell us something about ourselves. They speak not just of the one who created us but of what he created us *for*. As the author Nancy Pearcey puts it:

> *"We can 'read' signs of God's existence and purposes in creation ... It is evident that living beings are structured for a purpose: eyes are for seeing, ears are for hearing, fins are for swimming, and wings are for flying."*
> *(Love Thy Body, page 21)*

And periods are for... well, we'll get to that.

This idea that our bodies have a message for us is sensed, at least on some level, by non-Christians coming at this from a secular standpoint—even if the "message" they hear is something different to what God intended. For example, in her 2019 TED talk "Why can't we talk about periods?" the gynaecologist and *New York Times* columnist Jen Gunter says this:

24

"With oestrous [for a pregnancy], the final signalling to get the uterus lining ready comes from the embryo. But with menstruation, that choice comes from the ovary. It's as if choice is coded into our reproductive tracts."

This was met with a wild round of applause from the live audience, who, it appears, saw her line as supporting pro-choice. Whatever you think of the conclusion Dr Gunter has drawn (and, for the record, I think it lacks logic), the point for the moment is that she's drawn one.

And as Christians, that should come as no surprise. Romans 1 speaks of humanity as operating in this in-between state of both *seeing* the truth and *suppressing* the truth: "what may be known about God is plain" to us, but we "suppress the truth by [our] wickedness"—by our refusal to worship God as God (Romans 1 v 18-19). We look at our bodies and can't help but hear them speak—but because we humans are instinctive truth-suppressors, the words we choose to hear are our own.

But the good news is that there is a way to hear God's message more clearly. We're not just limited to his "general revelation"—we also have his "special revelation". The primary way that we hear God speak to us today is through his word, the Bible. Through Scripture the living God reveals himself—and, most importantly, he reveals how it is that we can be saved through Christ. There is no one more special than him. But we need God's Spirit to open our eyes to the truth, so that we can look at the world through the lens of Scripture and hear what it is that God has to say.

And that's the principle behind this book.

We'll look at our bodies—including our wombs—and see that they tell us something about God and about life in his world. Then we'll look at God's word and see that it tells us something about our bodies, about God, and about life in his world. We'll discover that when we take those two things together, they actually both make more sense.

So let's start listening.

WHAT PERIODS TELL US ABOUT GOD

We've already marvelled at the small miracle that is the menstrual cycle. We've already seen hints of a Designer with an intelligence that surpasses our own—a suggestion that if life in the body is an incredible gift, there must be a generous Giver behind our existence.

The opening chapters of the Bible don't just hint at these things; they declare them, right from the first words:

In the beginning God created the heavens and the earth.
(Genesis 1 v 1)

What follows in Genesis 1 is a riot of life and colour: vast seas and open skies; plants bursting with seeds; an explosion of birds and animals, jumping, climbing, teeming, swarming, swimming, squawking, squeaking.

Except it's not so much a riot as a carefully choreographed dance, with each space and creature carefully ordered "according to their kinds". Like seeing experienced couples rotating around a ballroom, each one is a joy to watch separately, but when they're viewed as a whole it's a spectacle: the dancers elegantly circling and turning past each other, rising and falling in time to the music of the seasons. And the whole thing gets more marvellous as God announces each new couple as they take to the floor: light and dark, earth and sky, land and sea, plants and trees, sun and moon, birds and fish, livestock and wild animals. As we read this first chapter of Genesis, it's as though we're invited to look on creation from heaven's perspective and join in with God's applause: it is good.

Until, all of a sudden, we're called onto the stage ourselves: man and woman.

> *Then God said, "Let us make mankind in our image, in our likeness, so that they may rule over the fish in the sea and the birds in the sky, over the livestock and all the wild animals, and over all the creatures that move along the ground."*
>
> *So God created mankind in his own image,*
>   *in the image of God he created them;*
>   *male and female he created them. (Genesis 1 v 26-27)*

Now, with God's image-bearers in place, creation is very good (v 31).

Today, as on those first days, all that God has made that we can lay our eyes on (and all that we can't) speaks of a Creator who is intelligent, imaginative, powerful, generous and good. That is true even of our very selves.

And this is true even of our most secret parts, including the parts we can't see. It will, I hope, continue to blow my mind that a hormone secreted in my brain can make something happen in my womb. My period may take me by surprise most months with a bright shock of red (I'm not a very diligent tracker), and my menstrual cycle may largely remain beyond my comprehension—but it's not beyond God's. He knows it all, because he made it. And it's just one tiny piece of all that he has designed inside my body, let alone beyond it. He is *that* knowledgeable, *that* creative, *that* powerful, *that* good. He is, frankly, unfathomable.

Admittedly, that's definitely not where my mind normally goes when my period arrives. My thought process does not jump to "wow" and "praise God". But it could, and it should, and maybe I would feel better if it did. After all, when the psalmist considers that God "created [his] inmost being", that's exactly where his mind goes: "I praise you because I am fearfully and wonderfully made" (Psalm 139 v 13-14). And the more we learn about our bodies, the more there is to appreciate.

That's not to say that periods *themselves* were necessarily part of God's original very good creation (although that's an interesting question—one which you can join me in wrestling with in the Appendix on page 111 if you want to). But it *is* to say that in our periods, we experience a vivid monthly reminder of the complex createdness of our bodies.

And when we look at our bodies through the lens of Scripture, what can we do except worship our Maker?

WHAT PERIODS TELL US ABOUT OURSELVES

Our bodies don't just tell us something about the Creator—they also tell us something about us, and the amazing purpose he's created us for. And once again, Scripture sheds light on the reality around us:

So God created mankind in his own image,
in the image of God he created them;
male and female he created them.

God blessed them and said to them, "Be fruitful and increase in number; fill the earth and subdue it. Rule over the fish in the sea and the birds in the sky and over every living creature that moves on the ground."

(Genesis 1 v 27-28)

The first humans are "blessed": they are the happy recipients of God's overflowing love, favour and generosity. Unlike all that's been made before them, they're created in God's image. And with that blessing comes a specific mission—what's sometimes called the "cultural mandate" (v 28). These verses have a whole load of implications, but for the purposes of this book we'll notice just two things.

First, *our bodies are good.* They are a fundamental part of who we are as humans. When Adam meets Eve for the first time, he declares that she is "bone of my bones and flesh of my flesh" (2 v 23); not, as we might write it, "soul of my soul" or "heart of my heart". It's not that the human bit inside us is merely *housed* in a body. We're not *trapped* in a body in this life, waiting so that we can be free of it in the next. No, humans are *embodied* souls, and will continue to be so in the new creation (when our bodies will be made perfect).

There's something *physical* about our humanness, our creatureliness. To be sure, we are more than our bodies… but we cannot be without them either. It's all bound together: mind, body, soul—whole. And like the rest of creation, our bodies are *good*.

This is especially important to remember as we consider the subject of periods, which for so many of us come with painful or shameful associations. We'll get to these in the chapters the follow. And it's also important to remember in a culture which tends to see our true selves as distinct from our body. These verses remind us that our biological sex is not an irrelevance; it's part of God's design from the very outset.

Scripture's emphasis on bodies is also why, as Christians, periods really are worth thinking about. They are not beyond the scope of theology; nor are they somehow so gross as to be beneath the category of a discipleship issue. Since our bodies are important, and since our female bodies are doing something particular (bleeding, or not bleeding when they're meant to be bleeding), then we should expect that this will affect us physically, emotionally and spiritually, to one degree or another. We can't leave our soul outside the toilet-cubicle door any more than we can leave our bodies. God created it all, sees it all and cares about it all—and we can too.

And then second, *our bodies come with a purpose*. God makes humans male and female, distinct yet together, and tells them, "Be fruitful and increase in number; fill the earth and subdue it". *Go, fill the earth with other human beings*. Whether or not we fainted during the sex-education presentation, I'm trusting that we've all gathered how *that* happens. It takes a male and a female, distinct yet together. God gives humans the command and ingrains in their bodies the biological wherewithal to carry it out (including, in our case, ovaries, and a womb, and a cervix and a vagina which can do *all sorts of stretchy things* during labour).

This is backed up by our friend "general revelation". To paraphrase the quote from Nancy Pearcey above, eyes are for seeing, ears are for hearing, and wombs are for... growing babies.

And this is good too. If periods are biologically impressive, then the process of *growing a human being inside you* is on a whole other level (although yes, it also comes with a whole other level of pain too). Perhaps you've felt that sense of wonder when holding a tiny baby: this person was not, and now they are. And that bundle in your arms is no mere mammal but a person—a person who bears the image of our awesome God, with all the potential, purpose and privilege which that brings. Women's bodies have been built with the God-given ability to bring new life into the world—to take part in his creation as we "create" new humans in his image. It's almost as though that cosmic "stage" on which God choreographed the marvel of Genesis 1 has been shrunk down into our wombs, where the miracle happens in micro.

No wonder this design is declared "blessed" by God in Genesis 1 v 28. And in the pages of the Bible that follow, we read of woman after woman for whom motherhood was longed-for and celebrated: Sarah, Rachel, Leah, Ruth, Hannah.

And for the joy of motherhood we have to thank our friend, the menstrual cycle. In the words of my friend Holly:

> *"There's nothing I like about having periods. But since having my son two years ago, I definitely have a new appreciation for my menstrual cycle and how it enabled me to grow and carry a tiny human life. Being a mother has been so much more demanding than I ever thought it would be. But he is simply gorgeous, and I love him so much I wouldn't trade that for the world."*

One way to "read" our periods as they arrive, showing us that—as far as we can tell—things are generally running a-ok in there, is to remember "God made me as a woman with the ability to grow a baby. That's pretty cool."

Now, I realise I might have lost some of you there.

First, because sounding like you might be saying "a woman's purpose is to have babies" is pretty offensive to 21st-century ears. Second, because for many women, everything is not a-ok in there, and periods that are late, heavy, sporadic, absent or agony are sometimes a symptom of that. And as soon as you are trying to get pregnant, each new period brings with it a sense of disappointment that you're not—and perhaps a rising tide of grief and fear that you never will be. These are painful emotional and physical realities. We'll explore them in much more depth later, but we need to acknowledge them here. Sometimes we're rightly cautious about celebrating motherhood too much because, for a variety of reasons, not every woman will experience it (or even wants to). I'm almost 30 and single and, honestly, I'm not banking on having kids.

That's why I'm as relieved as anyone else that the message of this chapter is not simply "a woman's purpose is only or mainly to have babies". For one thing, it is man and woman together who are given the command to "fill the earth" (and neither on their own has all the necessary equipment). And it's the man and woman together who are given the second command to "rule over" the earth—a lifetime's work of building communities and creating cultures, not as individuals but as humanity. More than this, it's men and women together who in the New Testament are given the new mandate to "go and make disciples of all nations" (Matthew 28 v 19). This new mission to bring new *spiritual* life into the world—to "reproduce" disciples who are not only in the image of God but are being formed into the likeness of Christ—is what matters most.

So it's not *just* about babies… but nevertheless, babies are good. Bearing and raising children is good. Motherhood is good. Wherever we're at personally, it's right to celebrate the creative, expansive, reproductive power of the human body. And at the same time we can rejoice that, for God's people today, every believer finds privilege and purpose in playing their part in the creative, expansive, reproductive power of the church body (more on this in chapter 5).

Your body is incredible. Your female body is incredible. And every facet of its intricate design speaks of its incredible Designer.

So your menstrual cycle is more than a mess. It's more than a mystery. It's part of life in a female body, as an image-bearer who displays the glory of God.

CHAPTER TWO

So Much Pain

When Caitlin's periods are bad, they are really bad. If one arrives when she's at work or out and about, she knows she has just a few short hours in which to get home before the crippling pain starts.

And the vomiting.

And the diarrhoea.

Sometimes, she doesn't make it. One time, she ended up curled in the foetal position on the pavement a few hundred yards from her parents' house.

She and her husband joke about the array of hot-water bottles they've collected from around the country. Her period seems to have a habit of arriving unexpectedly when they're away—writing off days of their holiday and sending her husband on a mission to the local supermarket or pharmacy to buy this most unfortunate of souvenirs. And while they can laugh about it after the event, in the midst of Caitlin's periods—when the skin on her abdomen is red from the scalding temperature required to ease the pain—neither of them is smiling.

Caitlin first went to the doctors years ago. Her concerns were dismissed. Earlier this year, she tried again. She wrote out beforehand exactly what she wanted to say, including a list of symptoms; she was determined not to be brushed off again. The GP this time was far more helpful, and referred her to the hospital, where she's been booked in for a scan… in six months' time. In the meantime, she waits.

Bea is a little further down the line. When she's on her period, even the kids in her class can tell that something is wrong as they watch their teacher go grey in the face and double over in pain. She told me she'd had external scans, internal scans and, eventually, an exploratory operation that required two weeks off work. Bea was just desperate for some answers.

There weren't any.

The doctors discharged her. There was nothing more they could do. Her big fear is that she won't be able to have children in the future. The doctors don't know whether that will be the case because they don't know what the problem is. Sometimes Bea wonders why God is letting all this happen.

IT HURTS

There are a frightening number of things that can go wrong with your menstrual cycle—a collection of ugly step-sisters with ugly-sounding names: dysmenorrhoea (cramps), amenorrhoea (no periods), endometriosis, polycystic ovarian syndrome, fibroids, cancer and more. Problems manifest themselves in a number of ways: pain during sex, pain during periods, or periods that are too long or too short or too heavy or too frequent or unpredictably irregular. Infertility and miscarriage bring with them their own particular heartbreak.

Endometriosis is a condition that a growing number of voices are trying to increase awareness of. It's where the kind of tissue that belongs to the womb lining (the endometrium) attaches itself to other organs in the abdomen. So when it's that time of the month, and the hormone signal goes out to shed the womb lining, problems arise. The journalist Emma Barnett describes the pain as feeling "like iron chains were dragging my stomach down, pulling me towards the floor, as my bones ground against each other during what should have been a lovely easy amble around a [city] park" (*Period*, page 71). Endometriosis is estimated to affect up to 10% of women, but in the UK it takes on average 7.5 years to get a diagnosis (Endometriosis UK).

For some women, the menstrual anguish is mental rather than physical. Many women who struggle with depression or anxiety report that these feelings are more acute before or during their period. In addition to that, it's estimated that 3-8% of us suffer from premenstrual dysphoric disorder (PMDD)—intense depression, anxiety and/or irritability, which is tied to specific phases of the menstrual cycle (*Period Power*, pages 274-276).

These examples are extreme but by no means uncommon. Maybe you experience something similar, and that's why you've picked up this book. Or perhaps you exist somewhere lower down the scale compared to the women I've talked about so far—but still, periods *really suck*. Your pain doesn't have to be debilitating in order for it to be legitimately painful. Whoever you are and however acute your symptoms, at one time or another in your life—and, most likely, at many times in your life—you will know this to be true: being a woman *hurts*.

So what are we to make of this world of pain? Reflecting on her experience of a painful gynaecological procedure, the author Lynn Enright writes:

> *"Perhaps because we get periods—and periods are excruciating for so many of us—there is a sense that to be a woman involves pain, that it involves putting up with it ... Period pain is to be expected, to be endured, to be borne—with discretion and even good cheer ... We bleed each month—and that is normal. We are in pain each month—and that is normal. We give birth to a baby, sweating, wailing, stretching, tearing—and that is normal. Even when our pain is abnormal, it is often misunderstood or minimized." (Vagina, page 125)*

Enright's words express both a sense of sad inevitability at a woman's lot and an indignant outrage that it should be this way.

So why is it this way?

Just as in the last chapter, when we look in the Bible, we see it working in tandem with the "general revelation" of what we experience month to month. It affirms both the sad inevitability and the indignant outrage. But then it offers something more. Yes, this is how the world is. No, it's not how the world should be. No, it's not how the world will always be.

The Christian worldview doesn't promise to clear away every doubt and question that suffering raises. It doesn't have a specific answer for Caitlin or for Bea. But it does at least give their pain (and ours) an explanation, a purpose, and an end-date.

NOT EASY, BUT BETTER

At the end of the last chapter we left Adam and Eve looking out over a brave new world that was full of promise and potential. But paradise didn't last. The man and woman decided that they didn't want to dance to God's tune anymore—and in so doing turned the whole showcase into a shambles. They listened to the serpent's temptation, and they ate the one fruit God had told them not to (Genesis 3 v 1-7). The fall from innocence to guilt happened in barely a moment.

This story is so familiar to most of us that it's easy to lose sight of the force of it: the sheer ingratitude, the brazen arrogance, the outrageous selfishness, the reckless damage caused. I'm guessing we've all felt that force when others have spurned our good will. We've felt the white-hot indignation which wants to shake someone by the shoulders and cry, "How dare you?"

How much more so a holy God?

His judgment is not skewed in any way by limited knowledge or self-righteousness; it is settled and fair, but that makes it no less frightening. In the aftermath of mankind's rebellion in Genesis 3, we see this cosmic shoulder-shaking moment when God declares his curse on the serpent and the soil.

With God's words, the man and woman's blessed creation mandate—the glorious command to fill and subdue the earth—becomes the very thing that will suffer in the fallout. Yes, the man will still eat, but the ground will be unruly and the work will be hard (Genesis 3 v 17-19). Yes, the woman will still bear children, but not without difficulty:

> *To the woman [God] said,*
> *"I will make your pains in childbearing very severe;*
> *with painful labour you will give birth to children."*
>
> *(v 16)*

Each new life brought into the world will come with a cost. These two short lines gather up stories of women around the world and throughout history. We hear the echo of these words in everything that can go wrong in pregnancy and childbirth—and in the inevitable pain that's involved even when things go right. And we hear the echo of these words in our bodies with every period. From menarche to menopause—from first period to last—the whole process seems laboured and the whole system so prone to malfunction. As with childbirth, even when menstruation is "working", it often still hurts. The pain pictured here in Genesis 3 is not just physical but emotional—that word in the first half of verse 16 can also be translated "sorrow". Maybe you've had your share of that too.

Being a woman hurts. And the uncomfortable truth in Genesis 3 is that it is God who made it this way: "I will make your pains in childbearing very severe..."

At this point we may feel our own sense of indignation rising—this time, at God himself. *Why would you make it this way?* On average, a woman loses nine days' productivity per year to period pain. Far worse, 810 women die worldwide every day due to complications related to pregnancy or childbirth. Maybe we want to shout right back at God, "How dare you?"

Like I said, the Christian worldview offers no easy answers. But might they be better answers?

After all, consider the alternatives. Even if we were to decide to wake up tomorrow as atheists, the facts of the matter mean that indignation is unavoidable—the question is merely who or what we direct it at. Lynn Enright points her indignation at dismissive doctors and the power of the patriarchy. But what hope does that offer to someone like Bea, who's reached the end of the road but is still no better? It offers no sense of meaning: no rhyme or reason for her pain, nor any hope in or beyond it.

"Why is it like this?" If we ask that question of a doctor about our symptoms, perhaps the worst thing to be told—as Bea has discovered—is "We don't know". An explanation is better than nothing, even if it's bad news. And if we ask that question in a philosophical context, we don't, if we're honest, want to be told, "We don't know" either. An explanation is better than nothing, even if it's bad news.

So here it is: humanity has twisted the order of creation to try to put ourselves on top, and now everything is bent out of shape. Nothing can be completely good when something so fundamental has gone so completely wrong. Nothing can be untaintedly beautiful in a world where humans have rebelled against their Creator—that in itself just wouldn't be right. Maybe it makes sense that it is arguably the most beautiful things that have become the most badly broken.

So we're right to feel sad and to feel indignant. It really isn't meant to be this way. But we're mistaken if we don't also grieve the reason that it *is* this way—the fact that it is sin that has spoiled God's good creation. And as we do that, we have to admit that we ourselves are part of the problem. It's not just Adam and Eve; we too are culpable.

This is *not* to say that there is a direct link between your sin and the severity of your periods: as though if yours are worse, that's because God is punishing you. Jesus was very clear that we must be very, very wary of drawing a line between a person's sin and their suffering (John 9 v 3; Luke 13 v 1-5). It would likewise be a mistake to suggest that God is punishing women more than men because Eve was somehow more to blame than Adam for what happened in the garden. It's not like that either (Romans 5 v 12). Nor does the Bible imply that it is inappropriate for women to seek out medical treatment, or to campaign for things to be better, or to take action against period poverty. We know from the life of Jesus that indignation at sin and compassionate action to relieve suffering are not mutually exclusive (Mark 1 v 40-42). If you're bleeding at times other than your period, if you're struggling with pain, or if your symptoms prevent you from living life as normal, *please talk to your doctor*. You don't just have to grin and bear it.

But this *is* to say that, in a general sense, suffering signals to us that the world isn't working. We women bear a monthly reminder of the fall in our bodies. That doesn't undo any of the truths we saw in the previous chapter about our bodies being the site of great creative blessing. We live with—we embody—both blessing and curse, joy and sorrow, love and loss. While some of us seem to experience more of the latter half of those pairs than others, none of us escape them completely, because the world is both good and fallen. Indeed, the Holy Spirit says through Paul that the "whole creation" is "groaning as in the pains of childbirth" (Romans 8 v 22)—in pain, yet with the hope of something better. And we can let our periods preach that to us every month.

BETTER YET, HOPE

An explanation is better than nothing, even if it's bad news. And better yet if there's hope of a cure.

And in this case, there is.

It's striking that a woman's body—this site of great blessing which has become a site of great pain—was also promised to become the site of great redemption. The Lord God said to the serpent:

> *I will put enmity*
> *Between you and the woman,*
> *And between your offspring and hers;*
> *He will crush your head,*
> *And you will strike his heel. (Genesis 3 v 15)*

God is promising Eve that, after many, many generations of painful childbearing, from one woman will eventually come a child who will "destroy the devil's work" (1 John 3 v 8); and in so doing, this "offspring" will free humankind from the power of sin. In this sense, "she will be saved through childbearing" (1 Timothy 2 v 15, ESV). God is promising the first humans that one day Satan will be crushed, the power of evil will be broken, and sin and all its effects will be expunged from God's creation. He will restore things to their proper order, and everything will work just so.

Stand where Eve stood for a moment, with the wreckage of paradise behind her and a pain she has never known but will become familiar with stretching in front of her. How precious these words of hope must have been for her. And these are words of hope for us, too. If you're one of God's people, there is an end-date on your suffering. You may feel worn down as month after month you experience the same pain, like a wheel that you wish could stop turning. You may feel hopeless, having exhausted all the medical options. You may feel dread or despair or just downright fed up. But you won't feel this way for ever. Your pain has an end-date—it's fixed on God's calendar already.

The snake-crusher has come. He's already put away your sin and made you spiritually whole. He's already dealt the mortal blow to the devil. Now all that's left for Jesus to do is to sweep up the mess on the day that he returns.

But notice again *how* God promised that he would do it in Genesis 3.

This snake-crushing champion did not come riding down on a horse from heaven. He came from the body of a woman, amidst straining and shouting, as Mary gave birth in a cattle stall in Bethlehem.

And when he grew up, this hero did not win his victory with a dignified show of strength. He won it on a wooden cross, with pain and panting, as he suffocated to death on a hill outside Jerusalem.

Here's how another prophecy, spoken by Isaiah in around 700 BC, described it:

> *³He was despised and rejected by mankind,*
>   *a man of suffering, and familiar with pain.*
> *Like one from whom people hide their faces*
>   *he was despised, and we held him in low esteem.*
> *⁴Surely he took up our pain*
>   *and bore our suffering,*
> *yet we considered him punished by God,*
>   *stricken by him, and afflicted.*
> *⁵But he was pierced for our transgressions,*

> *he was crushed for our iniquities;*
> *the punishment that brought us peace was on him,*
> *and by his wounds we are healed. (Isaiah 53 v 3-5)*

Here is God's answer to our indignant accusations that he doesn't care about our suffering—he came to bear it on himself, in the person of Jesus. He came to end the pain by coming through pain, into pain. Here is a Man of Sorrow for women of sorrow.

There is something very precious about this when we're feeling brought low. Jesus is someone who knows what it is to grimace and groan, to feel stricken and afflicted, to be held in low esteem, to experience something so painful that no one else seems to be able to look him in the eye.

All this means at least two things for how we see the world as Christians—and for how we experience our periods.

First, Jesus is with you in your suffering. Whatever your hurt—whether it's the agony of endometriosis, or the grief of miscarriage, or the emotional and physical toll of menopause, or something else—Jesus gets it. He doesn't simply do his best head-tilt-sympathetic-nod-must-try-and-fix-my-face-so-I-look-understanding pastoral counselling. He's familiar with pain. And as a Christian, you can know that he's entered into *your* suffering and taken up *your* sin, to guarantee you a future without either—an eternity of peace with God, with a body, mind and soul that are healed and whole. He's not the kind of man who is awkward or embarrassed about "women's problems" (Mark 5 v 34). Whatever you do or don't feel comfortable sharing in your small-group prayer times, there's nothing you can't share with Jesus in your personal prayer times. He sees. He knows. He's listening.

Second, God can do things with our pain. In God's way of operating, the most beautiful things that have become the most broken things are restored to become the very best things. That's what we see with childbirth in Genesis 3—the blessing became weighed with sorrow, but would ultimately be used to bring about redemption. That's what we see at the cross—"by his wounds we are healed" (Isaiah 53 v 5). And that's what we see in our own lives—sometimes only in the long view, but sometimes in the short view too. Look where Paul goes next with the childbirth image in Romans 8:

> [22]*We know that the whole creation has been groaning as in the pains of childbirth right up to the present time.* [23]*Not only so, but we ourselves, who have the firstfruits of the Spirit, groan inwardly as we wait eagerly for our adoption to sonship, the redemption of our bodies.* [24]*For in this hope we were saved* … [26]*In the same way, the Spirit helps us in our weakness. We do not know what we ought to pray for, but the Spirit himself intercedes for us through wordless groans.* [27]*And he who searches our hearts knows the mind of the Spirit, because the Spirit intercedes for God's people in accordance with the will of God.*
>
> *(Romans 8 v 22-24, 26-27)*

When we groan—whether in the pain and confusion of suffering or in the battle against sin—the Spirit knows just what we need. The Spirit himself is praying for us in accordance with the will of God, that we might be "conformed to the image of his Son" (v 29). Jesus is the very best thing in the universe. So to be like him is the very best thing for us.

It might be that we can't possibly see how that could be so in our circumstances. But that's the great thing—we don't have to. Even when we "do not know what we ought to pray for ... the Spirit himself intercedes for us" (v 26).

God can use all our experiences to make us more like Jesus in the present. I hope you can see ways in which he's done that—ways he's grown you in patience, humility, dependence, compassion, gratitude, love and all the many other beautiful qualities that Jesus exemplified in his life. If you can't see that, maybe ask a Christian friend—those close to us are often better at seeing how the Spirit has been at work in us than we ourselves are.

And through the process of pain, God is going to make us like Jesus in the future, too. Paul says that right now it's as though we're living in the labour ward—but one day the baby will be in our arms. We're straining towards "our adoption to sonship, the redemption of our bodies" (v 23)—the day when Jesus returns, and God's people and God's creation are totally restored: made new, free from sin and suffering in body, mind and spirit.

WHY BEING WEAK IS NOT (NECESSARILY) AN INSULT

So far, we've thought a lot about pain, but there's another word that it's helpful to think about in relation to our periods. Periods make us feel weak. Maybe reading that rankles—writing it certainly does, despite knowing the truth of it. That's because in our culture "weak" is an insult. We strive to be *strong* women.

This leads to an interesting dynamic in the conversation around periods, particularly when it comes to the concept of "menstrual leave"—the idea that employers should allow women time off during their periods or the opportunity to work flexibly around their cycles. 21st-century women aren't quite sure what to make of it. On the one hand, journalist Emma Barnett says that "it's just silly that women are still in a position where they are made to feel that the ideal worker body is male, and so any sign of femaleness must be concealed" (*Period*, page 129). Why should the way we work be set up to suit men best and not women? But on the other hand, she says that most of her friends "have wrinkled their nose in disgust at the idea of preferential treatment, or being treated as disabled in some way for the duration of their period" (page 124). It would place women at a disadvantage if they were seen as less employable than men. Even if firms did introduce menstrual-leave policies, "only women who aren't directly competing with men—or those who don't care about their progression and have nothing to lose—would take up such a policy" (page 127).

Which leaves us with a tension: the acknowledgement that men and women may have different needs versus the desire to compete on equal terms in all regards and excel. So which is it? Should I "own" my periods and fight for them to be acknowledged, or should I just power through as though they're an irrelevance?

It's a paradox we can see in so much of today's narrative around women's rights. And it's a paradox to which the Bible has a uniquely freeing—but countercultural—answer. Only the Christian worldview can resolve the tension.

This is because, first, in the Christian worldview weakness is not despised. "Weak" is something that most of us are desperate not to be. But not Jesus. He willingly became weak. Christians follow a Saviour who saved us through taking on weakness, and who now displays his grace and power in his people through their weakness (2 Corinthians

12 v 9). Here's a thought: have you ever noticed how, in almost every church, in almost every culture, in almost every part of history, the women outnumber the men—often by a significant margin? (If you're a single woman, you've *definitely* noticed.) I was pondering out loud to a friend once why that might be, and she said it was simple: "God chose the weak things of the world to shame the strong" (1 Corinthians 1 v 27). Might there be some truth in that? How, then, can we do anything but rejoice to be one of the "weak things" whom God has chosen?!

God loves to work through weakness. He doesn't let out a sigh when, yet again, we're struggling. He's a patient Father who helps us—not with an eye on his watch but with a smile on his face. Day by day he meets us in our weakness not with derision but with gentleness. Surely that should be how we meet our own weakness and that of others?

"But enduring pain is a sign of strength," you might argue. And yes, there's truth in that too. But might the way we brandish that idea reveal that we're being guided by a worldly dislike of weakness? Sometimes we're so desperate to appear strong that we need to be reminded that if it was ok for Jesus to feel and look weak, it's ok for us too. While pain is a result of living in a fallen world—it is, in itself, bad—there's a sense in which many of our weaknesses are simply the result of being creatures—they are, in themselves, neutral. Tiredness is a function of being human, not being fallen. Sometimes it's helpful to acknowledge the fragility of our bodies and the limits of our emotional resources. We are not God. We are created beings. We're not required to be limitless.

Second, in the Christian worldview, men and women are complementary to one another, not in competition with one another. The Bible is clear that in God's good design the two sexes are different, and sometimes we'll have different needs. That doesn't in itself leave women at a disadvantage. Granted, in a fallen world, which doesn't value all the things God values, it might. But in a Christian community, which loves the things God loves, it shouldn't. We can rejoice that women and men are different, yet still both good and both essential.

This is why Peter tells husbands to "honour" their wives "as the weaker vessel" (1 Peter 3 v 7, ESV). If we equate "weaker" with "worse", this is immediately an insult—but, as we've already seen, that's not how the Bible views weakness. Peter's words are probably a reference to the fact that, in general, men tend to be physically bigger and stronger than women. So much of modern life depends more on brains than on brawn that for many of us, in the absence of anything heavy to lift, this fact doesn't make that much difference day by day. But for some of us, there are a few days each month when we feel unmistakably like a weaker vessel. By instinct, we don't want to admit that to ourselves, let alone to anyone else. But what if we did? Well, in a Christian community such an admission of weakness ought not lead to a hierarchy with the strong person at the top, feeling superior. It should lead to the strong person getting on their knees to serve and "honour"—to raise up—the weak. And this dynamic isn't limited to male-and-female relationships. The New Testament is full of commands to those who are "strong" in whatever way to use that strength to serve the weak; it's full of exhortations to treat the church as a body, which is made up of different parts that are good at different things, but which all work together (Romans 14 v 1 – 15 v 2; 1 Corinthians 12 v 12-30; Ephesians 4 v 1-16).

Where this different-but-both-essential dynamic is in operation, it's so liberating. It frees us from constantly needing to try to prove ourselves and from thinking we've failed when we don't manage to. It frees us from feeling that we have to squeeze ourselves into someone else's mould— and, conversely, it also means that we don't need to feel bad about living out the stereotypes, as if that in itself is a crime against womankind. It frees us to be able to ask for help when we need it, rather than having to pretend like we don't. It means we can willingly and joyfully offer up our gifts and abilities in the service of our church, our neighbours and our families, however that might look. This isn't about settling for less but about playing to our strengths, if I can use that word. It means that we won't be crushed, or sidelined, or ignored if we don't fight our corner—we don't have to fight our corner, because we're being nurtured and valued and listened to already. It means we don't need to be out for ourselves all the time; we can simply aim to be all-out for Jesus.

That verse in 1 Peter ends by saying that both women and men are "heirs ... of the grace of life" (1 Peter 3 v 7, ESV).

Yes, there's a lot of pain. But there's even greater gain ahead.

CHAPTER THREE

So Much Mess

What's your most embarrassing period story?

When I ask my friend Emily that question, she tells me about a time she was having dinner with her new colleagues at a Chinese restaurant. She got up at the end of the meal and looked down at her seat with horror to see that blood had soaked through her trousers onto the fabric of her seat.

"What did you do?!" I ask, on the edge of mine.

"Well, I just pushed the chair back under the table and got out of there as quickly as possible." I can almost feel her cringing.

Emily hasn't had a period since she started taking the pill when she got married six years ago, and she's not sorry. "Mortifying…" "Embarrassing…" "Humiliating…". These are the words she keeps using, with increasing emphasis, as she thinks back to the time in her life when she experienced regular heavy periods: the hassle of going through ten sanitary towels a day, with almost hourly trips to the toilet required; the stress of sitting through a two-hour exam and worrying about whether she was leaking through her jeans; the embarrassment of coming on her period when she was staying with her fiancé's parents and having to tell her mother-in-law-to-be about the bloodstained bedsheets the next morning.

It's only after 20 minutes of the conversation (and only when I mention it) that she remembers that periods were physically painful. "Oh yeah," she says, as the memory dawns from some deep recesses of her mind, "and the *pain*…". For Emily, the physical pain has largely faded from her memory. But the feeling of shame? That comes flooding back as strong now as it was a decade ago.

The problem with periods is not just the pain. For many, it's not even mainly about the pain. Think periods, and we think—we feel—shame.

It's because periods have long been a source of embarrassment that they are shrouded in secrecy and surrounded by silence. Most of us go to great lengths to make sure that no one (except perhaps our closest friends) knows that we're on. Heaven forbid if some otherwise unsuspecting man should come to know it. That would be… embarrassing. So it's all tampons-hidden-up-shirtsleeves on the way to the toilet; and if we're caught without in the workplace, we send coded messages to female colleagues to see if they can help a sister out.

We learn this code young. When I was at high school, we used to ask our friends to "put the old man on"—the hand dryer—while we went into the cubicle to change. The idea that we felt the need to do this in single-sex toilets full of other girls who menstruated is now, with hindsight, a little strange. But then again, I can't claim to have grown out of the well-timed rustle in the toilet cubicle to coincide with a toilet flush two cubicles down.

There's a rising tide of voices saying that it's high time that we got over it. In 2015 Kiran Gandhi hit the headlines after she ran the London Marathon "free bleeding", saying, "I ran with blood dripping down my legs for sisters who don't have access to tampons and sisters who, despite cramping and pain, hide it away and pretend like it doesn't exist. I ran to say, it does exist, and we overcome it every day." And periods have continued to become more and more visible. Even the most recently made James Bond film almost featured a scene where a female agent threw a tampon in the bin. In the words of journalist Jonathan Dean, "Nothing shows how much Bond, and indeed the world, has changed more than a testosterone-filled blockbuster wondering if the time is right for a bit on periods" ("What Next for James Bond?", *The Sunday Times Culture Magazine*, 8th March 2020).

This really matters. Cultural taboos around periods lead to serious outcomes for women and girls around the world. A sense of embarrassment is what prevents many women from seeking medical help for gynaecological issues. Period shame leads teenagers in some countries to miss several days of school every month; in parts of India, as many as 20% of girls drop out of school altogether when they reach puberty. Even if our own shame manifests itself in less significant ways, we all know how it feels: terrible.

And the blame for centuries of taboos partly lies at the door of religion: "Unfortunately," writes the activist Nimko Ali, "these views have centuries of religious disgust to back them up" (*What We're Told Not to Talk About (But We're Going to Anyway)*, page 50).

WE NEED TO TALK ABOUT LEVITICUS

This leaves Bible-believing Christians in an awkward position—because right there in Scripture we find passages like Leviticus 15. Leviticus comes straight after Exodus's dramatic account of God's rescue of his people from slavery in Egypt. He brings them to Mount Sinai and gives them his law, outlining what life for his newly freed people is going to look like.

And for 50% of the population, for the greater part of their adult life, once a month it's going to look like this:

> [19]*When a woman has her regular flow of blood, the impurity of her monthly period will last seven days, and anyone who touches her will be unclean till evening.*
>
> [20]*Anything she lies on during her period will be unclean, and anything she sits on will be unclean. [21]Anyone who touches her bed will be unclean; they must wash their clothes and bathe with water, and they will be unclean till evening. [22]Anyone who touches anything she sits on will be unclean; they must wash their clothes and bathe with water, and they will be unclean till evening. [23]Whether it is the bed or anything she was sitting on, when anyone touches it, they will be unclean till evening.*
>
> [24]*If a man has sexual relations with her and her monthly flow touches him, he will be unclean for seven days; any bed he lies on will be unclean.*
>
> [25]*When a woman has a discharge of blood for many days at a time other than her monthly period or has a discharge that continues beyond her period, she will be unclean as long as she has the discharge, just as in the days of her period. [26]Any bed she lies on while her discharge continues*

will be unclean, as is her bed during her monthly period, and anything she sits on will be unclean, as during her period. ²⁷Anyone who touches them will be unclean; they must wash their clothes and bathe with water, and they will be unclean till evening.

²⁸When she is cleansed from her discharge, she must count seven days, and after that she will be ceremonially clean. ²⁹On the eighth day she must take two doves or two young pigeons and bring them to the priest at the entrance to the tent of meeting. ³⁰The priest is to sacrifice one for a sin offering and the other for a burnt offering. In this way he will make atonement for her before the LORD for the uncleanness of her discharge.

³¹You must keep the Israelites separate from things that make them unclean, so they will not die in their uncleanness for defiling my dwelling-place, which is among them. (Leviticus 15 v 19-31)

What's your initial internal reaction to reading that? Confused? Outraged? Ashamed? Here's mine: *Really, God? Unclean for one week in four, or possibly more, for something that is entirely natural and healthy? Why? What's your problem with periods? Do you just hate women?*

So where do I go from there? How do I navigate the tension between my instinctive reaction on the one hand and, on the other, my belief that God is good and that the Bible is his word and that he loves me as his daughter? What's a woman to do with a passage like Leviticus 15? Here are our options:

1. *Just try to ignore it.* The whole of Leviticus is pretty wild (as is, if we're honest, a great deal of the Old Testament).

So we just don't read it that often, if ever. But given that you've just read 13 verses of it, ignoring it is now pretty much off the table.

2. *Try to diminish the offensiveness with cultural context.* We could point out that many, many other cultures and religions—both at the time Leviticus was written and since—have taboos and rituals around menstruation. So if our God hates periods, at least he's not the only one. It's also worth knowing that in ancient Israelite society, women probably had fewer periods in their lifetime than most of us do now. Girls got married soon after puberty, were encouraged to have lots of babies, and weaned them later—and both pregnancy and breastfeeding usually preclude periods (Gordon Wenham, *The Book of Leviticus*, page 224). This helps—but it doesn't make the principle itself seem any less unfair.

3. *Try to reason it through with biblical context.* (To be fair, this is always a good thing to do when it comes to the Bible.) As far as uncleanness goes in the book of Leviticus, menstruation is pretty minor. Someone who touches a menstruating woman is only unclean until evening— perhaps a matter of hours. No sacrifice is required, only washing (v 22—the sacrifice of verses 29-30 refers to the "abnormal" bleeding of verse 25). There's not even a command for the menstruating woman herself to wash, just the people who come into contact with her; all verse 19 says is that "the impurity of her monthly period will last seven days".
And it's not just women who are rendered unclean by (for want of another term) their "reproductive discharges".

These commands for women in verses 19-30 mirror similar ones for men in the first part of chapter 15, both in severity and consequences:

a. Verses 1-15: "unusual bodily discharge" from a man's reproductive organs (this refers to an abnormal discharge: it is serious, and unclean)

b. Verses 16-18: an "emission of semen" (that is, normal and less serious, but still unclean)

c. Verses 19-24: A woman's "monthly period" (normal and less serious, but still unclean)

d. Verses 25-30: A "discharge of blood for many days at a time other than her monthly period" (abnormal and more serious, and unclean)

The conclusion to the chapter in verses 32-33 shows us that these instructions belong together: "These are the regulations for a man with a discharge, for anyone made unclean by an emission of semen, for a woman in her monthly period, for a man or a woman with a discharge, and for a man who has sexual relations with a woman who is ceremonially unclean". So, we can tell ourselves, these instructions do not discriminate: both men and women are made unclean by their reproductive discharges.

4. *Shrug our shoulders and reassure ourselves that these laws don't apply to us now.* This is true too, up to a point. These words don't apply to us today in the same way that they did to women in ancient Israel. You and I are not unclean when we are on our periods.

But all the same, these are words about which the psalmist cried, "Oh, how I love your law!" (Psalm 119 v 97). And which Paul, writing to New Testament Christians, described as "holy, righteous and good" (Romans 7 v 12). And since God is unchanging, whatever these laws tell us about his character is still true today. We can't read the Old Testament and think to ourselves, "I'm so glad God isn't like that now". He most assuredly *is*.

5. *Resign ourselves to put up with it.* We might not like it, but the Bible says it. So we accept that it's true, even if we can't agree that it's good, and we tell ourselves that since Jesus died for us and all that, we'll keep following him. But while there's something to be said for shelving our tensions with particular parts of Scripture and focusing on what's most important, that's always in the hope that one day we'll be able to take it off the shelf and appreciate how good those parts are. Here's an opportunity to do just that.

We can't just explain this away or pretend it's not there. And if we were to try to, we'd miss out. The rest of Scripture assures us that there is something precious—something holy, righteous, good and loveable—to be found in Leviticus 15, and so there must be. But what is it?

CLEAN AND UNCLEAN

Let's go back to that word which glares at us repeatedly from this passage: "unclean". It's used a total of 18 times in 13 verses, the word reproducing on the page before our eyes as uncleanness spreads from woman to bed and chair and pots and pans and other people. Unclean. Unclean. Unclean.

The COVID-19 pandemic has given us all a taste of what it's like to live in a world of "clean" and "unclean". Suddenly we became careful about what we touched when we were out and about. Ordinary objects like doorhandles, card machines and restaurant menus took on a new threat. The virus was unseen and potentially deadly. We learned to avoid crowded places and refrained from hugging the people we loved because anyone could be contagious—including us.

To be "unclean" in Leviticus was not a statement on hygiene. It's not that a woman on her period (or a man with a discharge) is dirty. Nor is being unclean sinful *per se*. A woman on her period is not *guilty*: "Uncleanness establishes boundaries of action, but as long as these are not transgressed no guilt is incurred" (Wenham, page 220). Elsewhere in Leviticus (for instance in chapter 20) God lists actions, such as adultery and incest, which *do* incur guilt and should be punished. But having a period isn't one of them.

In Leviticus, things (and people) are described using the categories of holy and common, clean and unclean. "Holy" is what God is, as are the things that are set apart for his service. Everything else is "common". Common things are either clean or unclean.

Most of us already know a little bit about how this worked for the Israelites when it came to food. Some animals (like sheep and cows) were "clean", and therefore ok for the Israelites to eat. Other animals (like pigs and prawns) were "unclean", and so could not be eaten. Again, these categorisations were less about food hygiene and more intended as a picture of a bigger reality. The Israelites were God's people. They'd been brought through the Red Sea— their own kind of "baptism" (1 Corinthians 10 v 2)—and now they were "clean". Life in the promised land would be a kind of re-creation of the original state of humankind in the garden: God's people enjoying relationship with him.

The Gentiles (non-Jews), however, were still stuck in the natural state of all humanity after the fall: they were unclean, corrupted by sin and separated from God. They were, therefore, separate from God's people too. That was one of the main points of the law: it set Israel apart from the nations around them.

So the clean/unclean dietary regulations were both a picture of this separation and a helpful reinforcement of it (since with all those hotdogs and bacon cheeseburgers on the menu, Mr Israelite wouldn't be going round to Ms Gentile's house for a barbecue anytime soon). That's why Peter's vision in Acts 10, in which he saw a load of unclean animals on a sheet and was told to eat them, was so revolutionary. The message was: *The gospel opens a way for previously unclean people (Gentiles) to be included in God's people.*

Anyway, back to Leviticus 15...

WE NEED MORE THAN "CLEAN"

While animals were permanently either clean or unclean, most other things—and people—could move across categories. Clean things could become "holy" when set apart for God. But they could also become "unclean". And unclean and holy *must not be near each other.* When it came to worship at the tabernacle, clean people could come to offer sacrifices in the outer courts. Once a year, the high priest could enter the Most Holy Place at its centre—the place of God's very presence—but only after consecrating himself through a set of rituals to make himself "holy". But unclean people could not come near the tabernacle at all. Hence the warning in verse 31: "You must keep the Israelites separate from things that make them unclean, so they will not die in their uncleanness for defiling my dwelling-place, which is among them." If unclean people and things came into God's dwelling-place among his people—if they came anywhere near the Most Holy Place—they would die or be destroyed.

As we read Leviticus, one fact becomes painfully obvious: in the course of normal life, people became unclean pretty quickly. No healthy woman of reproductive age could avoid it, no matter how hard she tried.

So why did God make it this way?

Well, we don't really know for sure. My best guess is that this aspect of God's law was intended to remind the Israelites that while they were in the privileged position of being his people, this was not the end of the story. It reminded them that sin was not just a problem "out there" with the unclean Gentiles. It was a problem "in here"—in their own hearts—too.

It is no different for us. In the words of the 16th-century Reformer John Calvin, "Corruption cleaves to the whole human race" (*Harmony of the Law, Volume 2*, comments on Leviticus 15). It clings to us. It's real, serious, and contagious. Even good, God-given things—the very best things, like sex and childbirth—are tainted by it, and so make an Old Testament believer "unclean" (Leviticus 12 v 1-8; 15 v 18). Without God's gracious intervention, the gulf between him and humanity is unsurmountably vast. We can't make ourselves clean and stay clean by just trying harder. Maybe the point was to communicate to the Israelites that all the washing and all the sacrifices were just a temporary band-aid. A more radical solution was required.

These verses are also a reminder that no part of life is conducted beyond the gaze of a holy God. Even this most intimate part of a woman's life—her period—is seen, anticipated and regulated. I can attend church on a Sunday on my period and leave again with everyone none the wiser, but a woman going into the temple would have died if she was on hers. Why? Because God was able to see that she was unclean. He saw the most intimate part of her—and sees the most intimate part of you too. Creepy? Obscene? It might seem that way at first. But then consider that God sees something more intimate than even our menstrual cycle. He sees what's in our hearts—his knowledge of us is that intense, that total. It really is unnerving—invasive even.

And when he looks inside us, he sees our true, natural state: unclean.

While there are certainly layers of unhelpful cultural taboos around periods, we're kidding ourselves if we don't admit that they're… well, messy. They may involve a relatively small amount of blood (less than 80 millilitres) but that sure is prone to finding its way to a disproportionately inconvenient number of unwanted places. "Yeah, I feel unclean on my period," says one friend—a rather matter-of-fact doctor—as we discuss this passage. "I don't think that's culturally ingrained. They really are just messy."

Perhaps that's partly why, in several places in the Old Testament, God uses the vivid picture of menstruation to talk about the uncleanness of his people's sin (for instance, Ezekiel 36 v 17 and Lamentations 1 v 8-9). A lot of people know the verse in Isaiah when he laments that "all of us have become like one who is unclean, and all our righteous acts are like filthy rags" (Isaiah 64 v 6). What fewer people know is that the filthy rags he's talking about are *menstrual* rags. Outside of Christ, even our very best good deeds—our "righteous acts"—are corrupted by our fallen nature. It's like offering a stinking sanitary towel to a holy God. Yes, that's a gross image. But that's how gross sin is.[2]

"Why should we be ashamed of something entirely natural?" is the logic underpinning our culture's "period pride" movement. But a Christian is someone who admits that there is plenty that comes naturally to them of which they are right to be ashamed. I *should* feel shame about some of what comes naturally. I'm not talking about my period (to be clear, again: periods are not something to be ashamed of). I'm talking about my self-importance, which holds others in contempt; I'm talking about my latent partiality and prejudice; I'm talking about my callous lack of compassion for other people's suffering; I'm talking about my lazy selfishness, which pretends that I haven't seen someone's need when in fact I can't be bothered to meet it. Those things all come naturally to me—and they're all things of which I'm ashamed, or should be. Perhaps this is what periods are an opportunity to remind ourselves of: the uncleanness of our hearts comes from deep inside of us and flows into our actions, seeping into even our best endeavours and relationships, and staining everything we touch (Mark 7 v 14-23; Isaiah

---

2 It's worth pointing out that there are probably some other reasons why periods in particular were regarded as unclean. It could be to do with the idea that "the life of a creature is in the blood" (Leviticus 17 v 11), and so spilt blood is a symbol of death (we'll come back to this theme in the outro—see page 105). It may also be because periods are a sign that you're not pregnant—and since God's purposes in the Old Testament were specifically tied to childbearing, this was cast in wholly negative terms (more on this in chapter 5).

64 v 6). We're powerless to stop it, even if we wanted to. It's natural. But it's so, so unclean.

So, yes, left to myself I'm an unclean woman. Not because I'm a woman. Not because I menstruate and blood comes out of me. But because "from within, out of a person's heart ... evil thoughts come—sexual immorality, theft, murder, adultery, greed, malice, deceit, lewdness, envy, slander, arrogance and folly. All these evils come from inside and defile a person" (Mark 7 v 20-21). In a typical month, I find that pretty easy to forget.

But, as uncomfortable as it makes me feel, I do need to remember it; because it's only when we've appreciated the depth of the problem—when we've felt appropriate shame not at menstruation but at our unclean spiritual condition—that we're ready to hear afresh the words of peace offered by our Saviour.

NO MORE SHAME

Travel some 1,500 years and 400 miles from Mount Sinai to the edge of the lake of Galilee, and from the book of Leviticus to the Gospel of Mark, and picture this scene:

> *A woman was there who had been subject to bleeding for twelve years. She had suffered a great deal under the care of many doctors and had spent all she had, yet instead of getting better she grew worse. (Mark 5 v 25-26)*

Here is a woman suffering from the kind of abnormal lengthy gynaecological bleeding described in Leviticus 15 v 25-30. We don't know what her exact condition is, but we can imagine that, like many gynaecological issues, it is painful and exhausting—she has "suffered a great deal under the care of many doctors". Perhaps the search for a cure was worse than the original cause.

But worse than the pain is the shame. This is more than a leak on a chair in a Chinese restaurant. This woman has been ceremonially unclean for twelve years. What were you doing twelve years ago? Under the laws of Leviticus, that means twelve years without sharing a bed with her husband (if she had one); twelve years without enjoying the embrace of another; twelve years without coming to the temple to worship. Twelve years of exclusion and shame.

And now there's no hope of a cure. Her money is all spent, but the bleeding doesn't stop. She never wakes up better, and often she wakes up worse. Those stubborn red stains just keep on appearing, morning after morning, day after day.

Then she hears of a miracle-worker called Jesus, who has been healing great crowds of people with otherwise incurable illnesses. And she feels a glimmer of hope. Could he... *would he*... do that for her? Surely no self-respecting Jewish man will want anything to do with her. But she's desperate—it's been *twelve long years*. So she decides to chance the crowds to reach him, hoping that no one recognises her as an unclean woman who should be avoiding busy places:

> *When she heard about Jesus, she came up behind him in the crowd and touched his cloak, because she thought, "If I just touch his clothes, I will be healed." Immediately her bleeding stopped and she felt in her body that she was freed from her suffering. (Mark 5 v 27-29)*

In the blink of an eye, the pain goes and the bleeding stops. Imagine the relief as your heart soars in a moment of realisation that you're healed. But that euphoria quickly gives way to gut-clenching fear…

> *At once Jesus realised that power had gone out from him. He turned round in the crowd and asked, "Who touched my clothes?"*
>
> *"You see the people crowding against you," his disciples answered, "and yet you can ask, 'Who touched me?'"*
>
> *But Jesus kept looking around to see who had done it.*
> *(v 30-32)*

Picture her: heart in her mouth, head bowed, desperate not to meet this man's eye in case he can tell from her face that it's she who has touched him and it's she who has made him unclean. What will he say if he finds out? Will he turn on her in anger or turn away in disgust? She can't bear the thought of being exposed in front of all these people.

But Jesus won't stop looking for the culprit. It's only a matter of time before she's found out. So she steps forward, falls on her knees, and opens her mouth.

> *Then the woman, knowing what had happened to her, came and fell at his feet and, trembling with fear, told him the whole truth. (v 33)*

Perhaps there's a pause—a moment of stunned silence from the crowd. All eyes are on Jesus.

> *He said to her, "Daughter, your faith has healed you. Go in peace and be freed from your suffering." (v 34)*

The woman opens her eyes. She can see the dust in front of her face just fine. But are her ears deceiving her? There is no hint of anger or disgust in his voice, and his words are ones of love and acceptance: "Daughter, your faith has healed you. Go in peace and be freed from your suffering."

DAUGHTER...

When we come to Jesus, these are his words to us too.

"Daughter..." No longer are we held at a distance, kept outside the camp. We're brought into the embrace of God, loved unconditionally and cherished as the apple of his eye. How is that possible for someone so unclean? Because...

"Your faith has healed you." When we come to Jesus, believing that he can heal our sin and reaching out to him by faith, that's what he does. He makes us clean by the power of his cross, where he took our spiritual uncleanness upon himself. And he's so great a Saviour that just a fingertip faith is enough for our sin to be wiped away and for us to be given all that Jesus offers.

"Go in peace and be freed from your suffering." Jesus gives peace and freedom. He brings peace between us and God instead of conflict, and he restores peace within us. We're freed from all that we need to be ashamed of. Our sins have been forgiven, and our status in Christ is secure. We don't need to feel crushed by other people's expectations or live in fear of their judgment. We don't need to be ruled by our own internal monologue of self-loathing. Jesus has seen the worst of us and has loved us enough to die for us anyway.

"Daughter, your faith has healed you. Go in peace and be freed from your suffering."

That's the last we read of this bleeding woman in Mark's Gospel. How we'd love to know what happened next. We'd love to witness the scenes where she goes back home or starts to rebuild her life after her encounter with Jesus.

But in another sense, we get to do one better than read about it. As women who have been set free by Jesus, we get to live the rest of her story ourselves.

LEAVE IT WITH HIM

When it comes to period shame, there's a ditch on both sides of the road.

On one side of the road is the feeling of unnecessary shame. The shame that stops some of us from rustling around in the toilet cubicle takes on bigger, more serious proportions for others. I'm talking about the shame that stops us from seeking medical help when we need it. The skin-crawling awkwardness that stops us from having an honest conversation with our husband or giving the real reason for our absences to the HR team at work. The embarrassment that stops us from allowing another sister in Christ from bearing our burdens in this area.

And it's not just periods—so many of us feel shame in so many areas of our life as women. The self-loathing we feel when we look at ourselves in the mirror and wish that we could crawl out of the skin that we're in and hide in a dark place where no one will find us. The cringe-inducing conversation which keeps us awake at night as we replay it in our minds over and over again.

I'm not saying you have to talk about your period (or your hormones or your fertility or whatever else comes under the category of "reproductive health"). But don't not talk about these things because you're ashamed. And when you need to, but you can't quite bring yourself to, take a deep breath as you remind yourself of this: in Christ, God has called you his daughter. He delights in you. He has made your body good. He has already seen the worst of you and yet he accepts you, inside and out. He desires your good. And nothing anyone else says or thinks or does can take that away from you. Nor can anything you tell yourself alter that. This is what we need whenever we feel shame—period-related or otherwise. And this is what will enable us to "laugh at the days to come" (Proverbs 31 v 25), rather than living in embarrassment and fear.

There is a ditch on the other side of the road, though—and it is the attempt to erase shame as a category altogether. The "period power" rallying cry is part of a broader call that says it's time for women to stand up, stop apologising, and unleash our true and fabulous selves on the world.

But the Bible would have us beware the extremes of this kind of thinking. That's *not* to say that campaigning for better menstrual health and education, and the removal of stigma, isn't a good thing—it is. It's a compassionate response to suffering and inequality. But it *is* to say that always equating "natural" with "good" will lead us into all kinds of mistakes, and that it's worth remembering that shame is an appropriate response to our sinful thoughts and actions. Feeling that kind of shame is a good thing, if it leads us to the cross. *Only* Jesus can remove shame. Attempts to throw it off ourselves won't last; we'll be sat in the mud again before too long—if not in this life, then in the next one. But Jesus *does* remove that shame, at the cross. If you have good reason to be ashamed today, take it to him, reach out to him, and leave it with him.

Christian women don't have to be superheroes who look within and boast in our power; we're daughters of God who look to Jesus and rejoice in his.

CHAPTER FOUR

So Many Feelings

Imagine seeing one of those ice-cream shops in a quaint English seaside town on a hot day while you're on holiday. The bell above the door rings as you open it, and the person in front of you steps to one side to reveal that behind the glass-fronted counter are 24 tubs of... vanilla ice-cream. Row upon row of identical pristine cream-coloured mounds. "I'll have the vanilla, please," you say with confidence. As you take your cone out of the shady shop and into the sun, you have your first taste. It's sweet. It's pleasant. It's... well, vanilla.

There's something to be said for that peculiar ice-cream-shop fantasy. It would be a lot less stressful than a normal ice-cream parlour—especially if you have children in tow. There are no decisions to make and no risks to take. You know what you're getting, and you get what you know. A world where every ice-cream flavour was vanilla would be perfectly unobjectionable (assuming you like vanilla ice-cream).

But at the same time, you would miss out on so much. The dazzling array of tempting colours and flavours; the "I'll have pistachio today, and maybe tomorrow I'll come back and try the mango sorbet" sense of anticipation; the "let me try a bit of yours, and you can try a bit of mine" exchange with whoever you're with. Think of the flavours that you'd never get to experience: the zing of raspberry, the depth of dark chocolate, the crunch of honeycomb that gets stuck in your teeth.

Yes, a world where everything was vanilla would be perfectly unobjectionable. But it's just not as good as a world of different flavours. There's a lot to be said for variety.

IN CELEBRATION OF (SOME) EMOTIONS

In a chapter about the emotional side of the menstrual cycle, our minds might immediately jump to the negative. (Although granted, in this particular chapter, your mind might jump to *Why on earth is she talking about ice cream?*) In other words, think "periods" and "emotions", and we usually think PMS (premenstrual syndrome)—those times of the month when we are prone to feeling angry, irritable, sad or overwhelmed. And, yes, we'll get to all that. But first, it's worth celebrating the fact that God has designed us in a way which means that *not every day is vanilla*. Not every day feels the same. And that's a good thing.

There's a wonderful depth and variety to our moods and emotions. One day we're cheerful, bouncing down the pavement with a spring in our step. Another day we're determined, putting one foot resolutely in front of the other. Another day we're contented, moseying along at our own pace. And most days, we manage to feel three things at once, like a three-scoop ice-cream sundae in which the flavours all run into each other.

Just as God has made a natural world that changes colours with the seasons, he's made humans to feel an extraordinary range of emotional experiences. And he's given us language that enables us to communicate and share those emotions with others, giving us the opportunity to resonate and empathise and truly connect with people. Indeed, he's given us whole bodies with which to express ourselves: faces and frames that reveal so much about what's going on inside.

As in chapter one, we can't help but stand back and marvel. What an incredible gift it is to be human. What a marvellous thing to be standing in an "ice-cream shop" full of multiple and varied flavours of feeling.

Of course, all that's true of everyone, not just those of us with a menstrual cycle. Our mood can shift over the course of a day or a week depending on *any number* of things—from how much sleep we've had, to how long it's been since we last ate, to the fight we had last night down the phone with our sister. Even seemingly trivial things make a more-than-trivial difference. And big things make a big difference, shaping how we feel for weeks, months or even years.

The hormonal cycle adds yet another dynamic (as do the changes of puberty and menopause)—and it is a dynamic that, for many, is incredibly powerful. Many women find that rising oestrogen around ovulation makes them feel confident, assertive and sociable; whereas falling levels of oestrogen and progesterone in the days leading up to our period can make us feel anything from a little on-edge to like the sky is falling down around us.

Not long ago I asked one friend how her weekend was, and she answered, "I was so hormonal on Saturday night—I honestly felt like the world was ending. I couldn't stop thinking about how much I hated my job, how I hated my commute, how our flat was too cold, and how I hadn't cleaned the bathroom so I was a terrible wife. Normally I can reason myself out of that kind of thinking, but when I'm due on my period, it gets pretty dark. I was so sad I couldn't even watch *Strictly Come Dancing* [translation if you're reading this in the US: *Dancing With the Stars*]".

And that is where the ice-cream-shop image falls short; because, for all the delicious flavours of feeling that are available, there are others that taste bad—and even if we'd never choose them, we seem to get served them anyway.

And of course, how we're feeling often affects how we interact with the people around us. I'm guessing you probably know what it's like to spend a day snapping at your kids or glaring at your colleagues, only to come on your period a day or two later and think, "Ohhh… that's why I've been in such a foul mood". My friend Jess once fell out with her husband when she was due on her period and didn't talk to him for five days straight: "Not a single word," she says, with just the slightest hint of pride. "But it's not that I get annoyed over nothing when I have PMS. There's always a legitimate reason. But it's like, if my anger would have been at 3 out of 10 any other time, on the wrong day of the month the same incident will ramp it up to a 10."

I'm aware that I'm treading on sensitive ground here (as if I haven't done enough of that already…). For many women, PMS is a really difficult but winnable battle. For some, the symptoms are so acute as to be in the category of premenstrual dysphoric disorder and require much more help than a chapter in a book can offer. (If that's you, do talk to your doctor and a Christian who you trust.) For still others, it's just not an issue at all. The challenge for an author trying to address these things—indeed, for any human being trying to empathise with another—is that none of us can truly experience life in another person's skin.

But the Spirit *can*, in a sense—because he indwells you. And the Spirit of God speaks to you through the word of God. So that's where we're going next—we're simply going to walk through chapter 3 of Paul's letter to the Colossians and see how it helps us to walk through life on those bad-flavour days. Before we go any further, why not stop and ask the Spirit to show you where he wants to encourage and affirm you, and where he wants to challenge you, through God's words today? I can't tell you whether on any given day you've acted like a saint or a sinner or have simply done well to survive. I can't tell you which parts of what follows are pointed right at you, and which are less so. But the Spirit can. So ask him.

THINK HARD

Turn to Google for wisdom on managing hormone-related emotions or outbursts and the majority of advice you'll find essentially boils down to self-care, self-justification and self-acceptance.

The Bible would have us start in a different place. What it offers is no less comforting than any of those things, but rather a whole lot more: Christ's care, Christ's justification and Christ's acceptance of us. That's the place to start, whatever the struggle or sin that we're dealing with and on whatever day of the month we're facing it.

The first half of Paul's letter meditates on the supremacy of Christ and warns the Colossian Christians of the dangers of false teachers who could drag them away from the truth. Then, in chapter 3, he turns to focus on what living for Christ truly looks like in every sphere of life. And this is how he starts:

> *¹Since, then, you have been raised with Christ, set your hearts on things above, where Christ is, seated at the right hand of God. ²Set your minds on things above, not on earthly things. ³For you died, and your life is now hidden with Christ in God. ⁴When Christ, who is your life, appears, then you also will appear with him in glory.*
> *(Colossians 3 v 1-4)*

When I was discussing PMS with a friend who works as a mental-health nurse, she pointed out that there's a difference between thoughts and feelings. We often confuse the two. Feelings tend to be one-word concepts: sad, happy, anxious. Thoughts are the things we tell ourselves: "Nobody really cares about me" or "I really hate my job". Our feelings feed our thoughts, and our thoughts shape our feelings. Although we may often have little control over our emotional responses, it is possible to retrain our thoughts. Hence most modern therapies like CBT focus on a person's pattern of thinking, in an effort to change how they feel over the long term. That's not to say that changing our thinking is quick or easy. But the Christian has the Spirit working in them to change them—so that what would be impossible to do on our own becomes possible with his help.

Paul is very clear about the direction in which we should be training our thoughts: *set your hearts and minds on things above*. "Heart" here is less about emotions and more about affections—what it is that we love. If you were to take a random sample of what my heart and mind were set on during any given part of the day, the chances are that the result wouldn't come back "Christ". This is perhaps especially true on those days of the month when we're prone to introspection: when we get sucked into a thought spiral focused on how much we hate our circumstances, how few friends we have, or what a terrible wife/mother/daughter/friend/boss/employee we've been. (And none of it is going to get better. Ever.)

One response is to try to reason with ourselves that none of those things are true ("You've got a lovely home"; "You saw X just last night"; "You worked loads of extra hours last week, so you've earned yourself a break now"). In *Period Power*, Maisie Hill suggests standing up to your "inner critic" and giving it a good talking to, like this:

> *"Well, you know what, critic, I'm not taking that. I'm looking back over my diary and noticing all the wonderful things I've done. I know you think I'm lazy because I'm on the sofa in my joggers, but that rest is well deserved because in my Summer [the days pre-ovulation] I totally smashed it, and now I'm prioritising rest." (page 142)*

Which is great and everything, until… what if you've *not* "smashed it" this month? And who's the judge of "wonderful"? Rest is good—but surely not if we have to earn it first?

We need something more objective to look to than our own self-assessment. And that's exactly what Paul sets in front of us. He points back to Christ's death, resurrection and ascension to glory in history, and he says that, because we've been united to Christ by faith, those things have happened to us too: "For you died, and your life is now hidden with

Christ in God" (v 3). Jesus died on our behalf, so that our old sinful self is dead, buried, and dealt with. He rose on our behalf, to bring new resurrection life to our hearts. And now Christ is "seated at the right hand of God"—and our life is "hidden" right there with him. We can't see that spiritual reality with our eyes right now, but one day we will: "When Christ ... appears, then you also will appear with him in glory". And in the meantime our spiritual standing is safe; no one can ever snatch Christ's sheep out of his hand (John 10 v 28). Not even our inner critic.

So, says Paul in verse 1, *since this is already true, let it fill your vision.* There is nothing bigger or better going on than this. If Christ is where our life is, then our affections and mind should follow. Imagine someone who has gone overseas on a business trip and is longing to be back home with the person they love. They like to work out what time it is back home, and what their beloved will be up to right then. They count down the days until their return flight. The date is set, and the ticket is booked, and in the meantime they set their heart and mind on the one they love as they look forward to being back where they belong. That's how we are to be. We will be with Jesus one day. And until that day, we set our minds on him.

Which, in one sense, should be easy enough. But it takes a conscious effort of the will. Notice the commands here: "Set your hearts on things above ... Set your minds on things above." There are plenty of "earthly things" to absorb our attention, some of them legitimately. But I'm sure that on any given day or week you've got one or two things that your mind keeps circling back to, over and over again for 17+ waking hours. What those things are may change with your hormones and with the circumstances of your life, but there are always a few favourite topics. Wouldn't it be great to be a woman for whom the favourite topic was *Christ*? It would be a joy to be that woman, and it would be a joy to be around her. So, says Paul, "Set your hearts on things above, where Christ is ... Set your minds on things above, not on earthly things."

"Yes, yes, but *how*?!" How do we shake ourselves out of a hormone-fuelled, introspective thought spiral? Here is one practical thing that I've found has helped me. I read about it in Linda Allcock's book *Deeper Still: Finding Clear Minds and Full Hearts Through Biblical Meditation*. Sometimes, when I notice that an "earthly thing" has captured too much of my affections, I put a hairband on my wrist for a few days. Every time I notice myself thinking about that thing, I swap the hairband to the other wrist and ask God to help me set my mind on Christ, and I "preach" to myself who I am in him. Something about the physical action really does help to break the train of thought and draw a line in the sand—but it's the reminder to pray that is really powerful. Eventually the hairband will be removed for whatever reason (like, I need to use it in my hair), and I'll go on ok for a while. And then I'll notice else something askew in my thinking and say to myself, "Today is a hairband day". And on it goes again.

THIS IS A BATTLE

⁵Put to death, therefore, whatever belongs to your earthly nature: sexual immorality, impurity, lust, evil desires and greed, which is idolatry. ⁶Because of these, the wrath of God is coming. ⁷You used to walk in these ways, in the life you once lived. ⁸But now you must also rid yourselves of all such things as these: anger, rage, malice, slander, and filthy language from your lips. (Colossians 3 v 5-8)

These are brutally frank verses. And there's a strange kind of comfort in the fact that Paul has to tell Christians in Colossae to rid themselves of anger and malice and lust—because clearly they weren't rid of them up till then. So it's not just you who flips out at your kids in a bout of uncontrolled PMS rage that takes both you and them by surprise; it's not just you for whom ovulation plus the wrong kind of TV programme can leave your body tense with sexual desire and your mind racing in all the wrong directions. Christians since the first century have faced these kinds of battles.

It's also worth remembering that these two lists in verse 5 and verse 8 are not exhaustive—"whatever belongs to your earthly nature" sure is a big, catch-all category. In his commentary on this passage, Mark Meynell points out that "selfishness [is] the common denominator" of the sins listed in verse 5 (*Colossians For You*, page 130). And on those days when oestrogen is riding high and I'm feeling good, I know all too well that there is such a thing as being selfishly gregarious—how easy it is for me to walk into a room and act as though everyone in it exists purely for my entertainment.

At the same time, Paul is also brutally frank about what to do with these: "Put to death, therefore, whatever belongs to your earthly nature" (v 5). If our true lives are hidden with Christ—if he died for our sin—then the behaviours we previously embraced or at least tolerated are no longer fitting (v 7). We can no longer come running when these desires whistle. Instead, Paul says, *Wage war against temptation. Don't let it overpower you. Put it to death.* It's serious: "Because of these, the wrath of God is coming" (v 6).

This is what we need to be reminded of if and when we're tempted to use our hormones as an excuse for sin. "Yes, I snapped at him—but *he* should try going through the menopause before he starts to judge," is an attempt to self-justify. "I'm genuinely sorry, but…" is a way of seeking to minimise what we've done. Yes, hormones *are* real, they *do* have a very real effect on how we're feeling, and it *is* helpful to acknowledge that. But sin is equally sinful (and repentance should be equally repentant) whatever the state of our hormones. Paul does not give any caveats here. He says of it all, *Put it to death.* PMS does not give us license to treat others badly. Nor does it mean that it's inevitable that we will turn into a she-wolf for three days a month (as we'll see in the next few verses).

It may also be that we need to wise up and get ready for the battle. Tracking our cycle and anticipating when the pressure-points are going to come may well help us to be prepared. Taking sin seriously sometimes looks like taking advantage of the common-sense, common-grace gifts of good sleep, regular exercise and proper nutrition. And if we're struggling with negative emotions, this is definitely a good place to start. Remember that we're whole creatures, body and soul—caring for one does wonders for the other. Taking sin seriously could look like being upfront with others so that they can pray for us and help us out practically to ease the pressure and minimise temptation. And taking sin seriously will *always* look like availing ourselves of the gift of the Holy Spirit, making sure we ask him to help us as we head into our day and praying throughout it for his power to be at work in us.

That's something we need to do every day. There's no point in our cycle that is temptation-free. But perhaps, by God's grace, that little ping of our period-tracking-app notification will be a prompt to renew our resolve: a fresh nudge to come to God for what we so badly need but so easily forget. Maybe that's God's grace in giving us a cycle; in gifting us a wonderfully complicated human body with scope to feel so many flavours. Perhaps if every day were vanilla—if every day brought the same battles—we'd lose the impetus to fight. Or maybe our hormones helpfully turn up the volume on the wayward desires that were there all along, so that we get the opportunity to see them more clearly. In the words of Bible teacher Nancy DeMoss Wolgemuth, "Anything that makes you need God is a blessing". Even PMS.

AN OPPORTUNITY, NOT JUST A PROBLEM

> [9]*Do not lie to each other, since you have taken off your old self with its practices* [10]*and have put on the new self, which is being renewed in knowledge in the image of its Creator.* [11]*Here there is no Gentile or Jew, circumcised or uncircumcised, barbarian, Scythian, slave or free, but Christ is all, and is in all. (Colossians 3 v 9-11)*

"I can't believe I let the hormones win," I'll sometimes think to myself when my period arrives after a few days of vile behaviour, or when Day 1 dawns and problems start to look a lot smaller. Sometimes it's easy to think as though my "PMS self" is someone distinct from my "real" calm-and-rational self.

Yet the Bible reminds us that the real battle is not actually between our "hormonal self" and our "real self". It's between our new self and our earthly nature. That's equally true whether we're on an oestrogen high or in a progesterone slump. It's not that we're at war with our bodies—Paul's not talking about something physical but spiritual (although the two do defy neat division). The important thing to remember is that our new self is now our true self. It's who we are and who we want to be. Yes, we're still living with an earthly nature that beckons us towards disobedience. Yes, we still struggle with fallen desires that love to jump on the back of any hormone that's going and ride it all the way into sin. But we nonetheless "are being renewed ... in the image of [our] Creator" (v 10).

Paul's big theme in Colossians 3 is church unity, not navigating PMS. But even so, knowing that God is at work to make us more and more like him can encourage us in at least two ways.

First, although some hormones may make it all the harder in our battle with sin, that doesn't mean that sin has to win. In the Spirit's power, you are free *not* to sin. And every time you hold back cross words instead of saying them out loud, every time you choose to bring your anxiety to God in prayer, every time you take a deep breath and choose to speak graciously instead of sulking, it is a victory. In that moment, you grew a little bit more Christ-like. So be encouraged! And the fiercer the battle, the sweeter the victory and the greater the change towards Christ-likeness—which is why PMS days are not just a problem to be navigated with as little collateral damage as possible but an opportunity to fight and win and change.

And second, you *are being* renewed—you're a work in progress. You're not there yet. So when we lose the battle, we don't need to lose heart. "Christ is all, and is in all" (v 11). And that gives us the power to carry out Paul's next command...

BEAR WITH ME (AND EVERYONE ELSE)

¹²Therefore, as God's chosen people, holy and dearly loved, clothe yourselves with compassion, kindness, humility, gentleness and patience. ¹³Bear with each other and forgive one another if any of you has a grievance against someone. Forgive as the Lord forgave you. ¹⁴And over all these virtues put on love, which binds them all together in perfect unity.
(Colossians 3 v 12-14)

I used to have a housemate who, after a particularly emotionally intense few days of hormone-related anxiety, would sometimes say, "Thank you for bearing with me". It stuck with me as a helpful phrase. It wasn't that she was apologising for being down—because she didn't have to. As we saw in chapter 2, weakness is not to be despised. Our human frailties—physical and emotional—are not something that have to be apologised for, because they're not something that need forgiving. Sad is a legitimate ice-cream flavour. We're human, life is hard, and not every day is vanilla... and that's ok.

But it was also a helpful phrase because it recognised that our weaknesses do need... well, bearing with. They impact on others. So Paul tells us, "Bear with each other" (v 13). Speak gently; be kind; reign in your own sense of entitlement. That's the call for anyone living with another person's hormones. In a funny sort of way, it was a joy to bear with my housemate (and, of course, there were days when she bore with me in turn) because it is always a joy to be Christ-like. Sometimes we beat ourselves up if we feel like we're a burden on others. But maybe God wants to use your weakness as an opportunity for someone else to embrace Christ-likeness as they bear with you.

Sometimes we confuse weakness with sin. Sometimes we excuse sin as weakness. The truth is that a lot of the time we act in a way that mixes sin *and* weakness—they are very hard to untangle. And we're prone to respond to our weakness in sinful ways. So we will sometimes need the second half of verse 13 as well as the first: "and forgive one another if any of you has a grievance against someone. Forgive as the Lord forgave you." When we get things wrong, we can simply come to Jesus, knowing that he bears with our weakness and forgives our sin, and so even when we are finding it hard to sort out which is which, it's ok. And it's this sort of humility that frees us to ask others for help with our weakness and for forgiveness for our sin.

EVERY DAY OF THE MONTH

I suggested that you start this chapter by asking the Spirit to prompt you personally—and that seems like a good place to end too. So think about these questions. What are the "flavours" that you typically experience throughout the month—good and bad? How do those impact the people around you? Are there things you need to repent of, to God and others? Are there things you need help with, from God and others? Where have you seen victories in your battle against your earthly nature, and where is the fight still most fierce? How might God be calling you to grow? Who could you talk all this through with—either for your own benefit or for theirs?

Whatever your answers to those questions, if you're trusting in Christ, you can know this for sure: you are one of "God's chosen people, holy and dearly loved" (v 12). On days when you feel low, the onus is not on you to look inside and dredge up some degree of self-love. You don't need to love yourself; you are dearly loved by another, outside of yourself. No other worldview can truly offer that.

And that, ultimately, is what will enable us to love others (v 14). That is what will empower us to wake up each day and clothe ourselves with compassion, kindness, humility, gentleness and patience—every day of the month, every month of our lives, until Christ returns and we appear with him in glory.

CHAPTER FIVE

So Little Time

A womb is a curious timepiece.

All other methods for marking time—sun, moon, stars, fitbit—are detached from us. But this one is part of us—literally built into our bodies. With each new period, another month(ish) has passed. Whether our period arrives with an element of surprise or a rush of relief or with crushing disappointment, "day one" is still a new beginning of sorts. We've reached the top of our own internal circle of life. And then the cycle begins again.

Until… it stops.

That's the thing. Our wombs don't just mark time month by month; they mark the seasons of life too. They provide a vivid transition from girlhood to womanhood, and then to whatever we can politely call what comes next—which is certainly no less womanhood but is nevertheless a transition significant enough that they call it "the change".

While most of us reading this will remember our first period, only some of us will know what it's like to have our last. If, like me, you find yourself in that first category, then it's entirely possible (even probable) that you don't really know what to expect of the menopause. After all, our culture doesn't really like to talk much about it beyond the obvious jokes and stereotypes, and there are no mid-life sex-ed classes for us to faint through.

Technically, the "menopause" is a single day, twelve months after your final period. In the UK and US, the average age for this is 51—but, like all the numbers in this book, that average masks a huge range of experiences. (Anything before 40 is considered "premature"; many times the cause is unknown, although some cancer treatments and medical interventions such as a hysterectomy will induce early menopause.) The symptoms that come before that day are the "peri-menopause", and anything that comes after that date is "post-menopause". But in popular parlance, we use the term "menopause" to refer to the whole period of time in which a woman experiences symptoms. This lasts around four years on average, although it can be as many as twelve.

When it comes to the symptoms, there are those that our culture likes to joke about: hot flushes and night sweats and hair in unwanted places. There are those that our churches are unlikely to talk about: vaginal dryness and reduced sex drive. There are those that are harder to put your finger on: a general brain fuzz that leaves you feeling not quite at your best, and mood swings and irritability ("I think I just felt angry for five years," says one colleague as she looks back).

Women who are going through the menopause also talk about the related emotional impact of everything that this stage of life typically brings: questions over their identity as their nest empties out; a sense of loss of femininity as their hair thins, and the fear that goes with it; a grief that their childbearing days are over, or that they never began and now never will. Kathleen Nielson writes of speaking to a single friend who felt "that she was paying the price for goods she never got to take home. She felt the shut-down not only of body systems but also of dreams" (*Women and God*, page 109).

It's worth remembering that some women will sail through the menopause with few symptoms and little emotional turmoil. Many women say they feel a great sense of freedom and relief, not grief, at no longer having periods. But for others, menopause is an ordeal that makes monthly menstruation seem a walk in the park by comparison.

Maybe, if you're in the midst of the menopause, calling our wombs a timepiece sounds far too elegant. In reality, the cogs grind—and then they grind to a halt. And yet again, we feel that women get the raw end of the deal.

But what if there were another way of looking at it? Writing for India's *Elle Magazine*, the novelist Zadie Smith reflects:

> *"It is commonly thought that time is the particular enemy of women. Because we supposedly have so much to lose: our 'looks', our fertility, our cultural capital ... But there are other ways of looking at it. That women have timepieces built into their bodies—primarily 'biological clocks' and the menopause—signs that must eventually be heeded, signs that are, finally, impossible to ignore, seems to me at least as much gift as curse ... Without that dreaded 'biological clock', without the menopause, and with few honest mirrors in the culture in which to reflect themselves, what or who will tell a man that he is old? ...*

> *"The truth is ... age exists for us all. It comes to you whether you believe in it or not. And I am now very grateful to be in a body that reminds me every day of this simple human truth. Which is not to say age does not bring me sadness, that I don't sometimes mourn for my 27-year-old self, nor miss a certain version of my face, breasts, legs or teeth ... [But] I think on the whole, I'd rather be sad than deluded." (Elle India, June 2018)*

Zadie Smith isn't a believer, but in some ways she sounds like a modern-day version of the Preacher in Ecclesiastes: "All share a common destiny ... Time and chance happen to them all" (Ecclesiastes 9 v 2, 11). Her words echo those of Moses: "Teach us to number our days, that we may gain a heart of wisdom" (Psalm 90 v 12).

Our timepiece is a blessing if it tells us the truth that we'd so often rather avoid: we're all ageing. More to the point, we're all dying. Our womb may shut up shop first, but one day so will our bodies. It's as though the hourglass has been turned over for each one of us, and our periods—and the menopause—remind us that the sand is slipping through.

Zadie Smith says that she'd rather be sad than deluded. But what if those weren't the only two options—what if there were a way for your timepiece to give you a renewed sense of purpose, vision and hope?

When we look in the Bible, we find that there is.

WE'RE JARS OF CLAY—AND THAT'S OK

If, for whatever reason, you feel perplexed, downcast or distressed by your limitations, you are by no means the first. While he experienced neither menstruation nor the menopause, the apostle Paul certainly knew pressure, sadness and physical decay. He even coined one of the Bible's most evocative descriptions of how life in our bodies often feels: we are "jars of clay"—brittle and breakable (2 Corinthians 4 v 7).

The phrase comes in Paul's second letter to the Corinthians, which is an impassioned appeal to the church in Corinth to come back to the true gospel and to come back in their loyalty to him, a true apostle. In 2 Corinthians 4, he reveals the physical and emotional toll of his ministry. He is "hard pressed", "perplexed", "persecuted" and "struck down" (v 8-9). He is pressured, distressed, hounded and depressed (*The Bible Speaks Today Commentary*, page 171)—so much so that he goes so far as to say that "death is at work in [him]" (v 12). He feels the sand slipping through every day. Like any woman who's heard the sound of her biological clock ticking, Paul knows that his body is wasting away. That's the reality of life as a "jar of clay" (v 7).

But Paul is not ready to give up. He is "hard pressed on every side, but not crushed; perplexed, but not in despair; persecuted, but not abandoned; struck down, but not destroyed" (v 8-9). Although death is at work in his body, the "life of Jesus" is being revealed in it too (v 10)—which means that rather than sadness, there's joy; rather than delusion, there's determination. So in the verses that follow, Paul resolves to do three things—and we can do them too.

WE SPEAK

[13]It is written: "I believed; therefore I have spoken." Since we have that same spirit of faith, we also believe and therefore speak, [14]because we know that the one who raised

the Lord Jesus from the dead will also raise us with Jesus and present us with you to himself. ¹⁵All this is for your benefit, so that the grace that is reaching more and more people may cause thanksgiving to overflow to the glory of God. (2 Corinthians 4 v 13-15)

Despite the physical toll of his ministry, Paul continues to speak of Jesus. He believes that there is a life after this one (v 14), he believes that the Corinthians need to hear about it (v 15a), and his earnest desire is for God to be glorified (v 15b).

And so he speaks. His aim is "that the grace that is reaching more and more people may cause thanksgiving to overflow to the glory of God" (v 15). It's an expansive gospel vision—more and more people giving more and more praise and glory to God.

In chapter 1, we thought about God's commissioning of mankind to "be fruitful and increase in number; fill the earth and subdue it" (Genesis 1 v 28). *Go and have babies,* God said. It was an expansive vision—more and more image-bearers giving more and more praise and glory to God.

Under the old covenant, God's people grew primarily through reproduction. As the Old Testament unfolds we watch them grow from one childless couple, Abram and Sarai, into a nation that was the envy of the ancient Near East (albeit relatively briefly—1 Kings 10).

And that's partly why periods were viewed in such negative terms in the Old Testament. If God's promises were to be brought about primarily through child-bearing, then every period—every month in which you were not pregnant—was a month in which God's mission was not being advanced.

And since God's ultimate defeat of evil was going to be brought about by the "offspring" of a woman (Genesis 3 v 15)—a child from her womb—then every period marked another month in which you were waiting for the Messiah's arrival; and the menopause would have drawn a line of sorts under your part in God's purposes. What might it have felt like for Naomi to have experienced the menopause, having lost her two sons (Ruth 1 v 12)? Or for Elizabeth, who was "childless because [she] was not able to conceive," and, by the time we meet her in Luke's Gospel, was "very old" (Luke 1 v 7)? For these old-covenant women, personal and national sorrow were entwined.

But we are not in the Old Testament, and under the new covenant things are different. While childbearing remains a great gift, it's no longer the great emphasis. God's Genesis 1 commission is echoed in Jesus' Great Commission to his disciples: "Go and make disciples of all nations, baptising them in the name of the Father and of the Son and of the Holy Spirit, and teaching them to obey everything I have commanded you" (Matthew 28 v 19-20). It's an expansive vision—more and more people, from more and more nations, living as disciples of Christ. These verses encompass both making *new* disciples—engaging in evangelism and leading people to the point where they make a public commitment to follow Jesus as Lord (signified in baptism, v 19)—*and* the ongoing work of discipleship—since "teaching" someone to "obey everything" that Jesus has commanded doesn't stop at the baptism pool.

So for God's people today, this is the main way we bring life into the world: not by bearing children but by making disciples. Or rather, the call to bear children is part of a bigger mission; we are to model and teach the gospel to any children we are blessed with as part of the call to go and make disciples.

If we believe this, we will speak (2 Corinthians 4 v 13)—because that's how disciple-making happens.

It happens as we speak of Jesus, open up the Bible, or sing his praises to one another. It happens as we teach children at church or around the dinner table, and as we ask questions to draw out the heart of a hurting friend. It happens as we invite people to read the Bible with us or message them to see if they'd like to come to church. It happens as we share what's encouraged us from the passage at a Bible study or as we praise God for his goodness to us as we chat over how our week's been on a Sunday. It happens as we pray with and for one another; it happens as we plead with God for Christ's kingdom to grow and for Christ's people to mature.

We believe, and therefore we speak.

And we do it even while the clock is ticking. "Death is at work in us," Paul tells the Corinthians, "but life is at work in you" (2 Corinthians 4 v 12). In fact, it's as though he's pouring himself out for the gospel, causing the sand to press through the hourglass faster. The mission is huge. And every day counts.

And while each period no longer has the same bearing on God's redemptive purposes, it could, as one friend pointed out to me, become a cause for reflection. What disciple-making have I done this month? Where have I nurtured spiritual life? Have I played a part in bringing new spiritual life into the world?

Perhaps we need to learn something from the women of Old Testament Israel—and the many women today—

who longed for children and who therefore knew what it was to grieve every period. That challenges me: am I *that* emotionally invested in the call to make disciples? Do I long for it *that* keenly? Am I *that* desperate for God's kingdom to grow? I should be. But often I'm not.

I need to learn to mourn my spiritual fruitlessness. Maybe you do too. And maybe each period can serve as a fresh reminder to do that. We can take Day One as a moment to check our priorities and recommit ourselves to the Great Commission: to pray more fervently for the desire and the opportunities to speak of Jesus; to determine to make every day of every month count for his mission. "We also believe and therefore speak" (v 13).

WE REMEMBER WHAT IS UNSEEN

[16] Therefore we do not lose heart. Though outwardly we are wasting away, yet inwardly we are being renewed day by day. [17] For our light and momentary troubles are achieving for us an eternal glory that far outweighs them all. [18] So we fix our eyes not on what is seen, but on what is unseen, since what is seen is temporary, but what is unseen is eternal. (2 Corinthians 4 v 16-18)

When I ask Clare about the menopause, she says,

"I thought I knew what to expect when it came to the menopause. If anything, I was relieved to be getting on with it. And then the night sweats started. For a few weeks they were irritating rather than anything else. Then, like an avalanche, they hit full force. On the worst nights, I woke a dozen times, boiling. Sleep deprivation

*had its predictable effect: my brain was mush, my sense
of humour had gone walkabout and I spent my time
apologising in advance to my nearest and dearest for any
waspish comments."*

Clare doesn't need telling that "outwardly [she is] wasting
away" (v 16). She can see it with her own eyes and feel it in
her own body. But Paul says that there is something else going
on as we age that can't be seen in the mirror—we are "being
renewed day by day" (v 16). The same spiritual life that we seek
to cultivate in others as we speak is being renewed in ourselves.
Though our earthly bodies are temporary, God's work on our
character is eternal; though our earthly bodies give us trouble,
one day we will enter into God's glory for ever.

This is so important to keep hold of in a culture that
prizes the things we can see with our eyes—namely, youth
and beauty. Most ageing happens pretty gradually—we go
grey one hair at a time. But one of the reasons why the
menopause can be so upsetting is that it feels so final: so
definitive. It is an undeniable and unignorable physical
declaration that *you are getting old*. Our culture says that's
a bad thing—perhaps especially if you're a woman. An
analysis of the dialogue in 2,000 Hollywood film scripts
found that actors and actresses aged 22-31 had 28 million
and 28 million words of dialogue respectively. But for men
and women aged 42-65, it was 55 million words versus
11 million words (*Vagina*, page 180). It's no wonder the
average British woman spends over £70,000 ($92,000) on
her appearance over her lifetime.

But when it comes to speaking about and serving Jesus,
neither your age nor your gender is against you. In the

Bible's view of things, getting older—and certainly *looking older*—is not necessarily a bad thing. In fact, Titus 2 suggests that as we mature, there are *more* opportunities for disciple-making, not fewer, as we become the "older women" who are so crucial to teaching the "younger women" in every church community. Paul urges Titus, a younger church leader, to...

> *... teach the older women to be reverent in the way they live, not to be slanderers or addicted to much wine, but to teach what is good. Then they can urge the younger women to love their husbands and children, to be self-controlled and pure, to be busy at home, to be kind, and to be subject to their husbands, so that no one will malign the word of God. (Titus 2 v 3-5)*

While it's true that, whatever our age, we can always be an older woman to someone, Paul does seem to have something generational in mind here. So if you're at a stage of life where various changes have led you to wonder what your place is, Paul assures you: *It's right here, getting alongside younger women.* This is not something that Pastor Titus can do himself—he needs you. And they need you. The older we get, the more younger women we'll find around us and the more wisdom we'll have to offer them. Which means that as we move towards and through mid-life, our spiritual fertility can continue to increase.

As our timepiece shifts within us, moving us from one season to the next, it reminds us to use our time well. Maybe you're someone who feels a great sense of freedom at the prospect of the menopause—you relish the idea of being released from particular burdens or responsibilities, and entering a new season of life. That's great. These verses in 2 Corinthians 4 are a reminder to make that new season count for the things that really matter.

Or maybe that's not you. Maybe you're someone who's arrived at the menopause mourning the children you didn't have or the dreams that never materialised. Or you're a younger woman, and reading about the menopause has produced a sense of panic that you're running out of time to have the kids and realise the dreams—you feel the sand slipping through your fingers and would do anything to make it stop.

If that's you, don't miss this: "We fix our eyes not on what is seen, but on what is unseen, since what is seen is temporary, but what is unseen is eternal" (2 Corinthians 4 v 18).

As you look at your middle-aged friend with a bunch of children up-and-grown and a house full of photographs and more grandkids on the way, it's pretty easy to "see" what she's done with the last three decades. And yes, what a wonderful use of them. By contrast, maybe the fruit of your labour for that part of your life feels a lot less tangible. You can't identify your spiritual children with a DNA test; you can't weigh spiritual fruit in pounds and ounces. That doesn't make it less real or less significant. Even if it looks as though we haven't made any significant difference to anyone, looks can be deceiving. Much of what God is doing remains unseen by us in this life. Paul invites us to look beyond the here and now, and trust that, somehow, our efforts are producing "for us an eternal glory that far outweighs them all" (v 17).

The challenge for all of us, whoever we are and whatever season we're in, is to daily fix our eyes not on our ageing body or the earthly circumstances we can "see" but on what we can't see, but which is nonetheless what is most real and most reliable: on Christ's kingdom, and our place in it.

And Paul gives us another glimpse of that in the verses that follow.

WE GROAN FORWARDS

[1]For we know that if the earthly tent we live in is destroyed, we have a building from God, an eternal house in heaven, not built by human hands. [2]Meanwhile we groan, longing to be clothed instead with our heavenly dwelling, [3]because when we are clothed, we will not be found naked. [4]For while we are in this tent, we groan and are burdened, because we do not wish to be unclothed but to be clothed instead with our heavenly dwelling, so that what is mortal may be swallowed up by life. [5]Now the one who has fashioned us for this very purpose is God, who has given us the Spirit as a deposit, guaranteeing what is to come. (2 Corinthians 5 v 1-5)

Finally, we groan. It sort of feels as though we've been groaning all the way through this book, and so it's fitting to groan here, towards the end. Maybe all that talk of spiritual mothering made you groan a little too. It's yet another thing you're meant to be doing at a time when you already feel sapped of energy and under pressure from all directions—work, childcare, ageing parents. Maybe you're struggling to sleep or your hot flushes leave you feeling wrung out and exhausted. Yes, we groan. Life in an ageing body means we can't not.

But notice where Paul directs his groaning: "We groan, longing to be clothed instead with our heavenly dwelling" (v 2). This groaning isn't about wanting to go back to our slimmer, suppler, sexier body of yesteryear. This groaning is about wanting to go forward to our "heavenly dwelling".

Right now we're housed in a body that's like a tent (v 1), but one day we'll be given a resurrection body that's built like a house in all the right ways—permanent, safe, unshakeable, un-ageing, with no hint of shame or embarrassment attached (v 3). Eternity will not be a disembodied existence of floating around as a soul. We'll be raised to life in a new body that will be no less real than the one we're in now, but will be a whole lot better. Comparing the two is like comparing a house with a tent.

It's this prospect which gives Paul great confidence as he faces the dangers of his travelling ministry—because "if the earthly tent we live in is destroyed, we have … an eternal house in heaven" (v 1). And this prospect can give us confidence as we face the slow decline of age, too. (Or, indeed, the dangers of travelling ministry—who says it's too late to head to some far-flung mission field? You go for it, sister.) One day, what is "mortal" will "be swallowed up by life" (v 4). That's a day worth longing for, straining for, groaning for.

Our internal timepiece reminds us that we live in a tent, and that some day it will be taken down. But we have something else inside of us too; or rather, some*one*: "the Spirit [who is] a deposit, guaranteeing what is to come" (v 5). Paul's logic is that since God has already given us his Spirit, we can be sure that one day he will give us every other blessing he's promised us too—including new, perfect, eternal physical life.

The timepiece tells us we're dying. The Spirit tells us that we're living, and that one day we will *fully* live. Make sure you're listening to both. That way you'll avoid both sadness and delusion. Make sure you're groaning in the right direction—forwards, not backwards.

And since we're all called to groan for our heavenly dwelling— since *godliness looks like groaning*—you could even say that this puts women going through the menopause at an advantage over those of us who are currently enjoying the benefits of our relative youth or health (or maleness). And if that's where we're at, there's a challenge here for us to be compassionate and considerate towards our sisters who are groaning. "While we are in this tent, we groan and are burdened" (v 4). Hopefully this chapter—and this whole book—has given you a tiny window into what the women around you might be experiencing. But you'd be a lot better served by asking them. If a part of our family is groaning—especially if they're someone we have responsibility towards—we owe them more than cheap jokes or silent frustration. We owe them an ear that's ready to listen, a heart that wants to understand, and a mouth that's ready to encourage. After all, one day you'll be the person needing the compassion and encouragement.

The Christian writer and speaker Mel Lacy has described the menopause as a discipleship issue and a sanctification process. Speaking at a seminar on the subject, she said, "For those of us in the local church, this will be something that women around us are going through every week, every month, every year, and we *do* have something to say as Bible-believing Christians into the lives of those women … In the world, workplace employers are really paving the way in terms of caring for women in the season of menopause … But actually as a church I don't think we talk about it at all; it's a 'head in the sand' kind of thing" ("Walking with Women

Through the Menopause", Word Alive 2019). You could say something similar about menstruation more generally. Is it a discipleship issue that you need to take more seriously?

MAKE IT COUNT

When I started out writing this book in earnest, I made a fresh attempt at consistently tracking my cycle in the interest of research. At the suggestion of one of the books I'd read, I started a mood journal in a notebook: starting on Day One of my cycle, I listed the date and then wrote down a one-word summary of how I was feeling. The next day, I did the same on the next line underneath. Then with each new cycle, I started a new list next to it.

When Day One dawned the other day, I discovered I'd filled up the page with lists (well, I'd written the dates, at least—there were plenty of gaps where I'd forgotten to write in my mood). I pensively ran my fingers over the page, feeling the grooves of my heavy-handed biro markings—four months gone, just like that. Days of my life that have passed through the hourglass with barely a scrawl of my pen, never to be recaptured. What had I done with them, I wondered? Had I used them well? Maybe not. I thought over the work done, the wounds healed, the words spoken. Maybe I had.

And then I folded over the next page and wrote the date at the top. Mood: Good.

Day One. A new month, a new start, a new opportunity to love Jesus, to look out for others, and to make every day count for God's kingdom.

Nothing But the Blood

I remember once watching some low-budget advert on TV for laundry detergent. It featured a hapless man with a huge stain on his shirt, and a voiceover which listed all the stubborn stains that this detergent could deal with: tomato sauce, red wine, grass, blood…

Whoever I was with laughed: "Surely if you've got that much blood on your shirt," they said, "you've got bigger problems than getting your clothes clean".

But maybe that company was on to something. After all, a significant section of the detergent-buying market does regular battle with bloodstains. There's a sort of secret cleansing ritual that we learn pretty quickly around the ages of 10-12. Did your mother induct you into it too? Run your underwear through with cold water asap, use some soap if you need to, put it in the laundry basket and hope for the best. And don't wear your best knickers on those days.

We know it all too well: blood *stains*. I'm guessing most of us have a drawer full of period pants to prove it.

So I can't help but give a wry smile when I read the apostle John's vision of heaven:

> *There before me was a great multitude that no one could count, from every nation, tribe, people and language, standing before the throne and before the Lamb. They were wearing white robes and were holding palm branches in their hands … These are they who have come out of the great tribulation; they have washed their robes and made them white in the blood of the Lamb.*
>
> *(Revelation 7 v 9, 14)*

In a strange reversal of every time we've spent scrubbing at our pyjama bottoms in the bathroom sink, these people have washed their robes in blood in order to make them *white*. Which is what makes me laugh. Humanly speaking, that just isn't how it works.

But in the Bible, it kind of is.

We can trace the theme of blood through the landmarks of Scripture that we've already travelled past. In Genesis 4— right after the creation and the curse, which we looked at in chapters 1 and 2—Eve, "the mother of all the living" (3 v 20), has the joy of giving birth to two sons: Cain and Abel. "With the help of the LORD I have brought forth a man," she says (4 v 1). But just a few short verses later she experiences what is perhaps the worst heartbreak any mother could face: one son murders the other. The first family go from filling the earth to slaying each other as Cain bludgeons Abel to death in a field. Then the Lord comes to Cain and says, "What have you done? Listen! Your brother's blood cries out to me from the ground" (v 10). Abel's spilt blood speaks of sin and suffering and injustice.

Then, in Leviticus 16—right after "the period passage" that we looked at in chapter 3 of this book—we get the instructions for the Day of Atonement. This was an annual event when the sinful Israelites could be reconciled to a holy God through sacrifice, so that they could be "at-one". The priest would kill a bull for his own sins and a goat for the people's, and then sprinkle the blood over and around the ark of the covenant, before going outside to smear it on the altar. We might imagine the "Most Holy Place" at the centre of the tabernacle as shiny and clean; but in reality it was spattered with years'-worth of blood (we can assume, since there are no instructions about washing it off).

Atonement involved a lot of blood. Why? Because, God says, "The life of a creature is in the blood, and I have given it to you to make atonement for yourselves on the altar; it is the blood that makes atonement for one's life" (Leviticus 17 v 11). Our hearts pumping, blood flowing, oxygen circulating is what keeps us alive. Humans have known since Cain killed Abel that if you lose too much blood, you die. So it's no surprise that blood takes on such a significant spiritual meaning in the Old Testament. On the Day of Atonement, every Israelite knew, a goat gets it in the neck when it should be you. It's their life for your life; their blood for your blood. "The law requires that nearly everything be cleansed with blood, and without the shedding of blood there is no forgiveness" (Hebrews 9 v 22). With blood, sin is washed away. Without blood, the stain remains.

Then, in the New Testament, we get to see what it was all pointing towards. God's indictment on Cain is his indictment on all of humankind: "Their feet are swift to shed blood; ruin and misery mark their ways, and the way of peace they do not know. There is no fear of God before their eyes" (Romans 3 v 15-18).

And yet... "God presented Christ as a sacrifice of atonement, through the shedding of his blood—to be received by faith" (Romans 3 v 25). He died when it should have been us: his life for your life, his blood for your blood. And make no mistake—when he was nailed to that cross, Jesus *really did bleed.* If Abel's blood speaks of sin, Christ's blood speaks of redemption.

Just like in the Old Testament, the atonement that Jesus has won is about more than reaching a ceasefire—it's about God making it possible for us to be close to him. Now "we have confidence to enter the Most Holy Place by the blood of Jesus ... let us draw near to God with a sincere heart and with the full assurance that faith brings, having our hearts sprinkled to cleanse us from a guilty conscience and having our bodies washed with pure water" (Hebrews 10 v 19, 22). This is our reality right now: Jesus has thrown the doors wide open and welcomes us in to fellowship with God. And this time, it's permanent.

As we reach John's vision at the end of the Bible, we're given a glimpse of what this reality looks like. Behind the scenes of the apparent chaos of this world, God is gathering a crowd around his throne. In Revelation 7 v 9-14 John sees not just one or two people, not just three or four thousand, but "a great multitude that no one could count, from every nation" (v 9), standing before God's throne and wearing spotless clothes which have been made clean "in the blood of the Lamb" (v 14). There are no stains, no shade of discolouration, no grey-ish patches. These are royal robes that will never be stained by sin again.

I love how one (beautifully graphic) old hymn picks up on this imagery:

There is a fountain filled with blood
  Drawn from Immanuel's veins;
And sinners, plunged beneath that flood,
  Lose all their guilty stains.

Revelation 7 is a scene of untarnished unity and joy and wondrous celebration. That is what Christ has achieved for us. And it's all by his blood.

Blood speaks. Right through this book we have seen how our periods speak both of curse and blessing, of groaning and gift, of pain and beauty, of Abel and Christ, of sin and salvation. They are, in a way, a jarring picture of what it means to live in a mixed-up world on its way to redemption. But one day the first part of each of those pairs will be taken away, and we'll be left only with the second; one day heaven will meet earth in the new creation, and God will wipe away every tear from our eyes (Revelation 21 v 4). Life in a woman's body might sometimes make us weep; but from that day onwards, our tears will turn into joy.

We know all that. But sometimes it feels so... other-wordly. Far off. Dreamlike. Unreal.

And that's why I'm kind of grateful for my period. From puberty to menopause, we women come into contact with blood pretty regularly. We see it and smell it and feel it; it gets into our sheets and under our fingernails. It's real. So maybe it can serve as a real reminder of a real day that is coming. A day when we and all God's people will be gathered round his throne, wearing spotless blood-washed white robes. A day when, in the words of that hymn, we'll have been "saved, to sin no more". A day when pain and fear will be banished. A day when Christ's blood will have the final word.

And that day will be as real to us then as the blood under our fingernails is real today.

So Many Questions

1. Did Eve have periods in the Garden of Eden? Will we have them in the new creation?

This is an interesting question because it really gets to the heart of the tension we encounter as we consider periods in light of the Bible's great story of redemption. In the framework of Scripture, are they positive or negative? Are they a symbol of life and healthy fertility or a symbol of death and frustrated fertility? If periods did exist pre-fall (but without any pain, obviously), then it's mostly the former. If, on the other hand, periods entered the world along with sickness, suffering and frustration, then it would largely be the latter. (That would also go some way to explaining why menstruation rendered a woman unclean in the Old Testament, as periods themselves would be tokens of the fall.)

Or here's another way to put it: in God's original design, with humanity having been divinely commissioned to "fill the earth and subdue it" (Genesis 1 v 29), would a woman have existed in a state of permanent fertility? Or would she only have been fertile (as we are) for a limited couple of days in a month?

If the latter, perhaps the cyclical nature of fertility is more akin to the cyclical nature of the seasons, which seem to have been part of God's original good design (Genesis 1 v 14). In which case, maybe in an unfallen world there was still a menstrual cycle, but the body reabsorbed the womb lining (as is the case with most animals, as we saw in chapter 1) rather than shedding it externally? We can only speculate.

I think we can say with more certainty that periods probably won't be part of the new creation. Jesus tells us that marriage won't be part of the new creation, since the greater reality to which it points—the perfect unity of Christ and the church—will have been brought to fulfilment (Luke 20 v 34-36; Ephesians 5 v 31-32). Plus, Revelation tells us that the full number of God's people will have been brought in (Revelation 7 v 4-8; 19 v 5), so there will no longer be the need to "fill" the earth via biological reproduction. All this would render a menstrual cycle unnecessary.

I could be wrong, of course. I guess we'll find out when we get there!

2. Is it ok for Christians today to have sex while the wife is on her period?

A friend of mine who is a pastor told me that this is a question he has been asked a lot over the years. It's one of those questions where the more you think about it, the less obvious the answer becomes.

Let's start with what we do know. It was unlawful for a man and woman in the Old Testament to have sex while she was on her period. This is stipulated in Leviticus 18 alongside a number of other sexual sins (mainly incestuous ones): "Do not approach a woman to have sexual relations during the uncleanness of her monthly period" (Leviticus 18 v 19). Leviticus 20 lists the appropriate punishments for each of these sins. In this case, "if a man has sexual relations with a woman during her monthly period, he has exposed the source of her flow, and she has also uncovered it. Both of them are to be cut off from their people" (Leviticus 20 v 18). (The eagle-eyed reader will notice that this sounds significantly more severe than 15 v 24, where "if a man has sexual relations with her and her monthly flow touches him, he will be unclean for seven days". The commentator Gordon Wenham reconciles these differences by arguing that this verse refers to something accidental rather than deliberate— that is, the woman comes on her period while having sex— see *The Book of Leviticus,* page 220).

So the question is: is the law prohibiting period sex still binding for Christians today?

As we saw in chapter 3, our relationship as New Testament believers to the Old Testament law is not completely straightforward. Jesus said that he came not to abolish the law but to fulfil it (Matthew 5 v 17); the ceremonial and ritual demands of the law have been fulfilled in his once-for-all sacrifice for sin. "We have been released from the law so that we serve in the new way of the Spirit" (Romans 7 v 6). The laws of Leviticus were given to the nation of Israel for a specific time—and certainly, since God's new-covenant people no longer exist as a nation state, the punishments listed in chapter 20 are no longer to be carried out. (See 1 Corinthians 5 for how Paul instructed the church there to deal with a case of incest.)

Yet the New Testament makes it clear that there are some laws which are still commands for Christians. (See again 1 Corinthians 5!) Jesus did not come to abolish the law, but he did significantly up the ante by pointing out that God's law is to govern our motives and thinking as much as our behaviour (Matthew 5 v 21-48).

So what are we dealing with here in Leviticus 18 v 19?

On the one hand, the prohibition in this verse against having sex on your periods sits alongside a list of other behaviours which an orthodox Christian sexual ethic would still regard as morally prohibited (for instance, "No one is to approach any close relative to have sexual relations", v 6; "Do not have sexual relations with your neighbour's wife", v 20; "Do not have sexual relations with an animal", v 23). So is having-sex-on-your-period, like committing adultery, wrong at all times and in all cultures? In favour of this view is the fact that at the end of the list in chapter 18, we're told that "this is how the nations that I am going to drive out before you became defiled. Even the land was defiled; so I punished it for its sin, and the land vomited out its inhabitants" (18 v 25). These behaviours weren't just wrong for the Israelites; they were wrong for the Gentiles living there before them.

On the other hand, here's what Kevin DeYoung says in a sermon on this passage:

> *"The key phrase in verse 19 is 'menstrual uncleanness.'*
> *Husbands should not have sex with their wives in their*
> *menstrual uncleanness. So the question is whether*
> *menstruation still makes a woman unclean."*

As we saw in chapter 3, the answer to that question is "no". So, concludes DeYoung...

"Cleanness still matters in the New Testament, but it becomes a moral category instead of a ritual one. Cleanness refers to those acts that are morally pure in God's eyes. So the abiding principle here is that whatever sexual activity makes you unclean is unfit for God's people. But blood loss no longer makes one unclean."
(thegospelcoalition.org/blogs/kevin-deyoung/sermon-on-leviticus-181-30-part-1/, accessed 20 October 2020)

One important consideration, though, is that to go against your conscience is sin (Romans 14 v 23): "If anyone regards something as unclean, then for that person it is unclean" (v 14). And to cause another believer to go against their conscience is also sin; it is unloving and destructive (v 20; see Luke 17 v 1-2). So if you or your spouse feel uneasy about this, the godly thing to do is to err on the side of caution.

3. Is it ok to use hormonal birth control to regulate my periods or treat pain?

Many women who are having issues with their periods are offered hormonal birth control by their doctor in order to reduce pain and regulate their cycle or stop it altogether. (Although strictly speaking, if you take the combined pill, then the bleeding you experience each month is a "withdrawal bleed" rather than a period.) Hormone replacement therapy (HRT) is a treatment that (in many cases) relieves symptoms of the menopause. Christians are free to use these to manage their symptoms, just as they are free to take advantage of any number of medications that we have available to us today. For many women, these are a lifeline. Praise God for these benefits of being alive in the 21st century!

However, if you've ventured anywhere near the internet on this subject, you're probably also aware that, like all medications, hormonal treatments can come with risks and side effects, and women's bodies respond differently. Some women's health practitioners are critical of the ease and speed with which hormonal contraceptives are prescribed, and maintain that for many women natural therapies are just as effective and overall more healthy (but just aren't as cheap and easy to administer as a prescription for the pill).

So, it comes down to a wisdom call; and wisdom will look different for different people. But, as in any decision, choosing the way of wisdom will involve thought and prayer, and often the counsel of others. Thankfully, Christians rest in the knowledge that God has numbered our days, and that our life (and health) is in his hands (Psalm 139 v 16)—so if you've prayed and sought counsel and opted to take the pill, you can take it in faith, not fear. "Whether you eat or drink or whatever you do, do it all for the glory of God" (1 Corinthians 10 v 31).

If you're married, it's also important to be aware that, of the seven hormonal contraceptives listed on the NHS website, six of them list thinning the lining of the womb to make it less likely that a fertilised egg implants itself as one of the ways in which they work to prevent pregnancy. If life begins at conception (that is, at the moment the egg is fertilised), there's a need to think through the ethics of this side of things very carefully. Every hormonal contraceptive is different, so it's vital to do the research. This may result in a decision to use other forms of contraception for "contraception" (that is, to prevent conception), so that any use of hormonal contraception for managing period symptoms is just doing that, and nothing more.

4. Should we call people who have periods women?

You may have noticed an increasing tendency in the media to talk about "people who have periods" instead of "women", so as to be (to use their terms) inclusive of trans men and non-binary people who have periods but who do not identify as women (and also of people who identify as women but who do not have periods). This became the subject of a Twitter storm in 2020 when the Harry Potter author J.K. Rowling questioned why an article headline referred to "people who menstruate" instead of "women". She tweeted, "'People who menstruate.' I'm sure there used to be a word for those people. Someone help me out. Wumben? Wimpund? Woomud?"

Why was this controversial? Because it conflicted with the view that was summed up in the response of the actor Eddie Redmayne to Rowling: "Trans women are women, trans men are men". Therefore, to imply that only women have periods is to suggest that trans men who have periods are not really men—or at least, not men in exactly the same way as natal men are (and the same for trans women who do not have periods). And this, in turn, conflicts with the way that a growing (and increasingly vocal) section of our culture thinks about gender: namely, that gender is not something biological but an identity that we express; and that to undermine another person's identity as they define it is deeply hurtful and offensive.

The narrative around this has changed quite dramatically in the last ten years. When I was studying an arts degree at university in the early 2010s, we were taught that sex is biological, but that gender is a social construct that is projected "on top", as it were—a set of norms and expectations (around dress and behaviour and so on) that are culturally defined. The confusion was that we used the same words—"man" and "woman"—when we were talking about both sex and gender.

Now, it seems, there's a growing expectation that those words belong exclusively to the category of gender. Some take it further and argue that sex itself is not binary—that is, that there are more than two sexes. (Sometimes, proponents of this view point to the existence of intersex people, who have ambiguous gender or chromosomal patterns.) Crucially, gender is primarily viewed as an innate identity from within that someone gives expression to rather than (as I was taught a decade ago) something that society imposes on us from the outside.

It's striking that despite all this, in other areas no one has a problem with equating "man" and "woman" with sex—when discussing relative mortality rates from COVID, for example. That's an indication that sex difference goes way beyond genitals—an increasing number of voices are showing how men's and women's bodies respond very differently to medications, for example (such as *Sex Matters: How Male-centric Medicine Endangers Women's Health and What We Can Do About It* by Dr Alyson J. McGregor). In other conversations, such as those around race, we readily acknowledge that the body we inhabit profoundly shapes the way we experience the world. And charities campaigning for the rights of women and girls around the world—including working to improve sanitation and access to menstrual-hygiene products, to end period stigma and to keep more teenage girls in school—rely on words such as "woman" to get their message across. I celebrated World Menstrual Hygiene Day 2020 by watching a video compiled by the charity Irise for their One World Period campaign. It first featured Dr Maria Tomlinson from the University of Sheffield, who told us:

"What really matters is that we all keep talking about periods … What also matters is the language we use to talk about periods. It's important that we use language that is inclusive, so words like 'people with periods' or 'menstrual products'. It's good to avoid terms like 'feminine hygiene' and 'sanitary products' because these words have negative connotations, that people who have periods are dirty, and also they're not inclusive of people of all genders."

The video then cut straight to Suzan Kerunen, a menstrual activist from Uganda, who said:

"Today I would like to lend my voice to the countless women all around the world in the campaign of 'One World Period'. It is every woman's God-given right to feel comfortable in their skin and their body, especially during their menstrual cycle. In my country, Uganda, up to 28% of young girls skip school monthly owing to their natural menstrual cycle."
(https://www.facebook.com/watch/live/?v=567345387258 279&ref=watch_permalink, accessed 26 October 2020)

The dissonance was striking. Who's to say who's right?

So that's what our culture is saying right now. But what does the Bible say? Well, I hope that this whole book has built up a picture of that with a lot more nuance than we have space for here. But fundamentally, when we look at Genesis 1, we see that God make mankind in his image, "male and female" (Genesis 1 v 27); and then immediately in the very next verses he tells them, "Be fruitful and increase in number" (v 28). Their maleness and femaleness is equated with their biological reproductive capabilities (in their perfect, pre-fallen state), not with a sense of identity or a set of social expectations. Gender is first and foremost given to them by a Creator, not performed by them.

And while this makes no sense—indeed, it is deeply offensive—to a culture which has rejected the idea that there is a Giver who has any authority over us (just as the first man and woman rejected that idea at the tree of knowledge, three chapters into the Bible), if we embrace the whole Christian worldview then this is actually wonderfully freeing. It frees us from having to live up to expectations or perform to type; it frees us from feeling obligated to break free from them; and it releases us from the constant difficulty of working out when we should be living up and when we should be breaking free. Not only that but, in Christ, we are promised resurrection bodies in a new creation where we'll be finally fully free from shame, stigma, inequality and any sense of internal conflict.

Since I left university, I've been preoccupied with the question "What even *is* a woman anyway?" I guess I wanted to know: am I doing it right? But being a woman is not something I have to do; it's something I am—a gift to be received. And my great hope as I've written this book has been that it will convince you and me both that being a woman is a good gift to have.

5. How should I talk to my children about periods?
In the course of writing this book, I've taken to asking friends for their first-period stories. Many were pretty mundane; others were memorable; a few were lost to the mists of time entirely. But almost all of them featured the same supporting cast member—their mother. Sometimes in the story she

was right there when they needed her; sometimes she was conspicuous by her silence; and sometimes, in line with her culture's traditions, she was attempting to arrange a party at which uncles would give her daughter gifts.

If you're reading this as a parent, my guess is that you probably already sense that you play a significant role in what your children know and how your children feel about periods—especially your daughters. The question is, how do we make sure those are the right things?

Since I have not experienced this aspect of life from the parental side, I asked a number of parents for their take. Three recurring themes came up.

Be open. A number of parents talked about how, when their children were young, they tried to cultivate the kind of relationship in which they and their kids could talk about anything and where questions were always welcome. Some women talked about how they didn't hide their own periods from their kids; so their children grew up knowing that their mum had them, and knowing something of what that meant. The consensus was that ideally "the periods chat" isn't a big reveal—it is, in fact, held over time, with small amounts of information being drip-fed into low-key everyday chats. That said, some parents made use of a book to read alongside their child (such as *Growing Up God's Way for Girls* by Chris Richards and Liz Jones). And some recommended having these kind of conversations while on a walk or in the car— side by side is always less awkward than face to face.

Be pro-active. As with sex, ideally the first person your kids hear about periods from will be you. It's therefore a good idea to find out when this is covered in the school curriculum. Most girls start their periods around age 12, but it can be as early as 8 or as late as 16; it's usually around two years after their breasts have started growing. Some mothers talked about showing their kids sanitary products, and making sure they knew where they were and what to do with them.

Be positive. It's one thing to make sure that kids have grasped the biological basics. But as Christians, we can use periods as an opportunity to affirm some of the big messages that we've thought about in this book: that our bodies are good; that God's creation of us as male and female is good; that motherhood is a high calling and a good gift—but that there's more than one way to be a "mother", too. We can remind our children that God wants all of us, male and female, to pour our energies into building God's church; that he uses all things, including pain, to grow us in godliness; and that when our bodies frustrate us now, we can look forward to the day when they will be raised in glory.

These are not the messages that the world will be giving your kids about periods. But they are messages that our kids— both daughters and sons—need to hear. But that doesn't have to happen in one single pre-puberty conversation. These are conversations you can continue to have as you disciple your daughter or son through their teenage years.

One final thing: most parents I consulted about talking to their kids about periods thought at the time that they hadn't done a very good job. Few of their children seemed any the worse for it several years later!

6. I'm a husband whose wife really struggles with her periods. What can I do?

For this question, I'll defer to the wisdom of someone who is both a husband and pastor: Rico Tice, Senior Minister at

All Souls Langham Place, London. When I first told Rico I was writing this book, he told me (once he'd got over the way the subject of periods had suddenly intruded into lunchtime conversation) that when he does marriage preparation with couples at his church, he always talks about periods. "I do believe that totally discounting this area leads to spiritual attack," he said seriously. He encourages a husband-to-be to talk to his wife about how her menstrual cycle tends to affect her, and to make a discreet note in his schedule of the days when she might be experiencing physical pain or finding things more emotionally intense. He encourages guys to avoid trying to make big decisions as a couple around that time, and not to jump to rash conclusions on the back of an argument but instead to come back to talk about the issues a few days later.

Most importantly, he encourages husbands to be a little more intentional about loving and cherishing their wives on those days.

What exactly does that look like? Well, it's going to depend on your wife. So ask her! If this is something she struggles with regularly—either physically, emotionally or mentally—have an honest conversation about how you can best love her through it. Don't assume she's overreacting or that she's only feeling something because of her hormones. Don't compare her with other women you know. Instead, "be like-minded, be sympathetic, love another, be compassionate and humble" (1 Peter 3 v 8). Encourage her to see a doctor where necessary (see page 42). Pray for her. If in doubt, be proactive about finding practical ways to serve. Wash the sheets, fill the hot-water bottle, and take the kids out for a couple of hours. And be encouraged that God has given you to one another to make you both more like Jesus through all that married life throws at you, including this.

7. I'm a pastor, and I've realised that our church has never, ever spoken about or supported women in this area. What can I do?

Ask some. Honestly, please do just that: ask some. Hopefully you have a bunch of Titus-2 older women who are already doing the work of discipling the women in your church. Why not ask how you could support them as they go about that? Paul tells Titus to "teach the older women" so that "then they can urge the younger women…" These women will have a much better idea of what would be appreciated in your particular context than I do.

Not every woman is going to want to talk to you about periods. Maybe you don't think it's appropriate to do so anyway. But if you want to be a pastor who is seeking to genuinely shepherd his whole flock—male and female—then maybe thinking a little more creatively about sermon application might be a good place to start. Rather than only referring to (rather bland) scenarios like "when work is stressful", why not also mention "the experience of menopause"? Or if you're listing things like cancer and car crashes as evidences of life in a broken world, why not also include endometriosis and period pain? Acknowledging struggles like these in small ways could have a big impact on your female hearers—and it signals that if their particular issue is a "woman's health issue", they can bring that to you for prayer and pastoral support without totally freaking you out.

Bibliography

Christian books

Linda Allcock, *Deeper Still: Finding Clear Minds and Full Hearts Through Biblical Meditation* (The Good Book Company, 2020)

Paul Barnett, *The Message of 2 Corinthians* (IVP UK, 1988)

Mark Meynell, *Colossians For You* (The Good Book Company, 2018)

Kathleen Nielson, *Women and God: Hard Questions, Beautiful Truths* (The Good Book Company, 2018)

Nancy R. Pearcey, *Love Thy Body: Answering Hard Questions About Life and Sexuality* (Baker, 2018)

Chris Richards and Liz Jones, *Growing Up God's Way for Girls* (Evangelical Press, 2014)

Gordon Wenham, *The Book of Leviticus, The New International Commentary on the Old Testament* (Eerdmans, 1979)

Secular books

Nimko Ali, *What We're Told Not to Talk About (But We're Going to Anyway): Women's Voices From East London to Ethiopia* (Penguin, 2020)

Emma Barnett, *Period. It's About Bloody Time* (HQ, 2019)

Lynn Enright, *Vagina: A Re-Education* (Allen & Unwin, 2019)

Maisie Hill, *Period Power: Harness Your Hormones and Get Your Cycle Working for You* (Green Tree, 2019)

Alyson J. McGregor, *Sex Matters: How Male-centric Medicine Endangers Women's Health and What We Can Do About It* (Quercus, 2020)

Acknowledgements

A huge thank-you to everyone at The Good Book Company for their partnership in the gospel, which I appreciated more than ever during the bizarre times of 2020; to the Publishing Board for taking a punt on this slightly strange idea; to Bethany and the marketing team; and to Carl Laferton, who edited this book with a commendable lack of awkwardness and who now knows more about my periods than most women's bosses do. Thank you for championing this book and for coaxing its author over the line, and for patiently enduring all the times I said I was nervous.

Thank you to all the people who bravely shared their period stories and ideas with me, and particularly to Cathy D., Katie B. and Tom W. for reading the manuscript and giving such helpfully detailed feedback.

Much of this manuscript was planned and written as I was enjoying the hospitality of my parents during the COVID lockdown. My thanks as ever go to them, my family, and my church family, for all their love and support.

COMPANY

BIBLICAL | RELEVANT | ACCESSIBLE

At The Good Book Company, we are dedicated to helping Christians and local churches grow. We believe that God's growth process always starts with hearing clearly what he has said to us through his timeless word—the Bible.

Ever since we opened our doors in 1991, we have been striving to produce Bible-based resources that bring glory to God. We have grown to become an international provider of user-friendly resources to the Christian community, with believers of all backgrounds and denominations using our books, Bible studies, devotionals, evangelistic resources, and DVD-based courses.

We want to equip ordinary Christians to live for Christ day by day, and churches to grow in their knowledge of God, their love for one another, and the effectiveness of their outreach.

Call us for a discussion of your needs or visit one of our local websites for more information on the resources and services we provide.

Your friends at The Good Book Company

thegoodbook.com | thegoodbook.co.uk
thegoodbook.com.au | thegoodbook.co.nz
thegoodbook.co.in